SMALL STEPS

SMALL STEPS

PAUL McNEIVE REVEALS HOW LOSING HIS LEGS DROVE HIM TO LEAD A €50m BUSINESS

'Everything is Possible'

Ballpoint Press

Published in 2012 by Ballpoint Press
4 Wyndham Park, Bray, Co Wicklow, Republic of Ireland.
Telephone: 01 2862272
Email: ballpointpress1@gmail.com

ISBN 9780955029899

Book design and production by Elly Design

Printed and bound by GraphyCems

Cover photograph by Mark Condren

I dedicate this book to my father,
James McNeive
And to my late mother, Pauline McNeive,
who taught positivity and confidence

CONTENTS

Paul McNeive is a business consultant, speaker and entertainer.

He is a Fellow of the Society of Chartered Surveyors and serves on the board of Ireland's National Rehabilitation Hospital.

He has three children and lives in County Wicklow, Ireland.

// **FOREWORD** //

You tend to remember where you were when you were asked for consent to amputate your legs.

I was in a narrow dark hospital isolation room which had seemed like a torture chamber for the previous four months. I was close to death. When three of the surgeons I had come to know so well appeared into my room together, grim-faced, and sat down around my bed, I had a fair idea what was coming.

In truth, I had been skilfully softened up for this over the preceding days by a couple of the nurses and my own instincts which were telling me that I was not going to survive much longer, as things were. The doctors were Mr. Prendiville (the head surgeon), Mr. Fitzpatrick (the man with the saw) and Mr. Lawlor, who had skilfully been grafting large amounts of my skin, from one part of my body to another.

"What? The two of them?" (I had been expecting just the right leg. There was already a few toes missing off my left leg, which I thought was bad enough).

"I'm afraid so, Paul. There is so much infection in your body, and so many grafts have failed that if we don't amputate your left leg as well, below your knee, then you might lose that knee too. And that knee is going to be important for you."

A long pause.

"Will I be able to walk again?"

"Yes, you will – using artificial limbs and crutches. The Rehabilitation Hospital in Dun Laoghaire does fantastic work."

I remember saying "okay so", and then just sinking back on my pillow as the doctors left. To some extent I was so sick, in so much pain and so drugged that I think I would have okayed their amputating my head. A nurse came in and squeezed my hand. Then she squeezed my morphine pump and I passed out...

And so, at age 20, my life changed.

Drastically and permanently. I had been battling to survive for four months. Now, every day of my life would be a challenge, a never ending series of obstacles to be overcome. I was going to have to work 10, 20, 30 times harder to achieve what I previously regarded as normality. For the first time in a carefree life, I would now discover if it was possible that I could drain further drops of energy and spirit from my heart and my soul, take even more kickings and still come back for more.

I was now "disabled".

Yes, later on as I stared out hospital windows, black fleeting thoughts of suicide crossed my mind, but never took root. I resolved to give these artificial legs, and life, my very best shot. And take it from there.....

Thirty years on I feel like I've been around the block a few times. Successes and setbacks, marriage, separation and three beautiful children. A lot of success in business and a lot of lucky bounces, mixed with moments of despair where just to keep going was a battle. Bereavement too.

I often wonder how my life might have turned out if I had never lost my legs. Would it have been any different? Would I have done much better? Why is it that some people can survive and thrive no matter what the challenge, whilst others flounder?

I wonder do we all have vast reservoirs of potential and strength, deep inside us, which we never use – because we don't realise they are there? Or because we don't have to? I'll share my thoughts on these questions as we go through the pages of this book.

Losing my legs propelled me into a whole new world of self-awareness and experiences. Along the journey of dealing with disability, I unconsciously found myself applying many of the insights and lessons I learned, into other areas of my life – including business. As I worked more and more as a business consultant and motivational speaker, I found myself drawn into writing down all of these experiences and thoughts – if only to get them clear in my own head.

I am far from being any type of business guru. Much of what I have learned was from making mistakes – and those are the lessons you don't forget. And I was fortunate in having some lucky breaks along the way. Like us all, I have strengths and weaknesses, but it takes many years of experience before you realise how those affect your business, your performance, and your impact on others.

In this book, I have set out many ideas and suggestions on how to improve your business and your own performance. I am not for one second suggesting that I am any good at all of these. I'm not. In fact, I'm pretty hopeless at some of them, but at least I'm aware that I can do much better, and I'm trying.

One of my greatest strokes of luck was that the most powerful period in my 30 years in business, when I had a good blend of experience and energy, coincided with the country's longest economic and property boom. I was lucky to find myself heading up a company with 250 staff. In the property business. It would have been hard to make a mess of it.

I love listening to new ideas about the world of business – from high level strategies to operational details, from the London Business School to picking up brilliant ideas over a pint. You can never stop learning. It takes many years to learn how to separate management bullshit from the "real stuff". You'll need a slice of common sense, an ability to observe the thousands of business interactions taking place around you every day – and to fine-tune your sense for how the customer or client is feeling about it.

Throughout 'Small Steps', you will find a theme of how positive consistent small steps in the right direction, can transform your business, and yourself. What worries me now is that I see lots of business owners under real pressure to survive. They focus all their efforts into cutting costs, reducing fees, special discounts, early birds etc, but do nothing about their customer service, which is probably more important. Then they're surprised when things don't change a whole lot. Here, I have set out to boil down over thirty years of life and business experiences into an easily read format which I hope will set you thinking.

Another reason for writing this book is that as a father of three children, two in college and one in secondary school, I constantly find myself being asked for advice as they face job interviews, college interviews and work on various business projects.

Sometimes, long after those discussions, I might wonder if I had explained myself well enough, or realise that I had forgotten something. I often wished I had it all written down somewhere and hopefully 'Small

Steps' will also prove of help to teenagers you know starting out in life, as well as to my own family.

Another motivation for me in writing this book is that it took me many years to fully come to terms with being 'disabled'. There were times when I was embarrassed and lost confidence. If any part of this book helps just one person with a problem to 'walk tall' and fight another round, then it will be worthwhile.

While my principles hold true in any market, (especially the crucial importance of customer service), they seem particularly suited to these tough economic times. But, here's the good news – despite the tough times, the standard of customer service in many business sectors – is fairly poor. At best, it's just okay. By definition, the standard of customer/client service, in **most** businesses, is **average**. Most businesses settle for the norm. And that, is your huge opportunity. Because a little extra effort, a few small steps, will soon raise you and your business above the average – and make you outstanding.

Never before have I felt such a sense of helplessness, particularly from people running small businesses. Business owners seem overwhelmed by a tsunami of problems, from lack of bank finance, to declining sales, to problems getting paid, to high costs, to new taxes. That's why it is now more important that we as individuals and organisations strengthen our ability to deal with adversity, to take whatever setbacks come along and then come back even stronger.

I started learning how to deal with adversity, in December, 1982...

// CHAPTER 1 //
RISING FROM THE ASHES

On the eleventh of December, 1982, I woke up hazily in the burns unit of a Dublin hospital. My head swam with the soothing sweetness of morphine. I was in a narrow room, with just one tiny window, high up in the wall on my left. Two days earlier I had crawled out of a burning car wreck, in flames. I had suffered serious burns to 76 per cent of my body to accompany various broken bones and a cracked skull. I looked through a mesh of tubes and wires at my hands, which were inside what looked like two plastic bags. They had swollen to about three times their normal size and had been cut open, to allow the fluids to drain out.

But my legs had got the worst of it. All of the skin had been burnt off my right leg which was also badly broken. It was now suspended in front of me, in traction, with large bolts going in one side and out the other. My leg was loosely wrapped in some type of aluminium foil, which magnified the sound of whatever was dripping out. Plop... Plop... Plop... Plop...

I looked to the other side.

On my left leg, the skin had been burnt away from my knee down. Some of my toes had disappeared. I remember that the room was very dark. And quiet. Slowly I became aware of a nurse sitting beside my bed on my right side. Apparently, the first thing I said was: 'Do you think I'll be home for Christmas?'

Little did I know – my battle with infection had just begun.

The hospital was called Dr. Steevens and back then housed the country's main burns unit. It was situated in Dublin city centre, on the south bank of the River Liffey and maybe a mile from the Phoenix Park, where Pope John Paul II celebrated mass for over one million people.

Many of my fellow residents were the last survivors of the Stardust Disaster, a fire in a Dublin nightclub, on St. Valentine's night, 1981, in which 48 young people died. The Burns Unit would be my home for the next four months.

Infection is the enemy for burns patients, as the loss of skin leaves you wide open to opportunistic bacteria. The burns may not kill you but a lot of severe burns victims die a number of weeks later from shock and infection. The medical teams' weapons are skin grafting (to replace the lost skin), antibiotics and an aggressive regime of hygiene. All of the patients are kept isolated in tiled rooms to prevent cross-infection. Visitors are kept to a minimum and must wear sterile gowns, hats and shoe covers.

The first few hours of every day brought almost unbearable pain. Once I had picked at my breakfast, two nurses would arrive in and start the process of changing all of the dressings which covered my legs. Large holes in my right leg were packed with long strips of cotton and these were then pulled out by tweezers the next day, like some kind of magician's trick. These agonies lasted for up to two hours. As soon as the nurses had finished, a physio would arrive and begin bending the fingers on my right hand, which had completely locked up. More agony. For a few weeks, the pain of changing dressings was so bad that I was brought every day to an operating theatre where I was semi-sedated. I soon knew off by heart the serial numbers printed on every light bulb over every operating table in the hospital.

Unbelievably, there was no aerial connection to the TV in the corner. Someone brought me a video player and an MTV recording and I watched Bonnie Tyler's video of 'Total Eclipse of the Heart', hundreds of times. I had a radio on my locker and I loved a new song called 'A Land Down Under', by Men at Work.

There was a constant stream of visitors, family and friends, who kept me going. At times like that, you find out who your friends are, and I had few, if any, disappointments. Many people went to extraordinary lengths to help out and show concern and support. Gerri Bourke, a girlfriend from schooldays, visited me every single night for months even though that involved four bus journeys every time. Every evening she brought me a red rose. On many occasions, I was too ill to have visitors, but every day the nurses would bring me in armfuls of parcels, presents, books, fruit and cards, that had been left behind by visitors. And always a red rose.

Over the first three months of 1983, I endured countless operations, mostly skin grafts, in an all out effort to save my legs. However I was getting weaker and weaker as I struggled from one infection to the next. By February, I could close my hand around my left thigh. I was anointed several times. I can still remember the cinnamon smell of the oil. Eventually, the bad bugs won the battle and in March, my right leg was amputated above the knee, effectively to save my life. A few days later, my left leg was amputated, below the knee. By that stage the cocktails of painkillers were being continuously pumped into my spine by epidural.

Another almost comical part of the routine were the efforts to get me to grow more skin as it was urgently needed somewhere else on my body. I was virtually force-fed a horrible concoction of raw eggs and chocolate in an effort to get me to regain some weight.

Every few days Mr Lawlor, the plastic surgeon, would carefully examine the unburnt parts of my body by carefully pinching his way around. As soon as he felt there was enough flesh available, I would be whisked off for another operation and the top layer of healthy skin would be 'peeled off' and grafted onto an area where I had no skin.

As a measure of how desperate the search for skin was, not long after my right leg was amputated even the remaining stump was used as a donor site for somewhere else. (By the end of all this, so much skin had been moved from my arms to my legs that I could be forgiven if at times I don't appear to know my arse from my elbow!)

Within days of the last amputations, I began to get stronger as the infection had been removed from my body. I was moved to a general ward – for company – after months of isolation. A treat I remember vividly was when I was wheeled to the room of Kevin Moran, the Manchester United and Ireland star. He had suffered a bad facial injury in a match in Dublin and had surgery in the hospital. He kindly agreed to chat with me and we spent ages talking football. I remember him telling me to watch out for a young Dublin lad who had broken into the United reserves. His name was Paul McGrath.

Strange as it seems, I think I only cried once during those months at Dr. Steevens Hospital. I was in a corner bed in a general ward and there were glass doors beside me with a view over the grounds.

It was lunchtime on a bright sunny day. A group of hospital porters started up a football match on their lunchbreak. I think it was the pure simplicity of what they were doing and the fun they were having. I loved playing football and my career had reached the glamorous heights of two years on the subs bench at Bray Wanderers. It suddenly struck deep that I would never be able to play a football match again – and this seemed to open the floodgates to months of pain, worries and the shock of what had happened to me. It all got on top of me and I cried hard for a long time.

On March 1st, I was transferred to the National Rehabilitation Hospital in Dun Laoghaire. As I left Dr. Steevens Hospital, a staff nurse who had been through many of the dressings agonies with me, unpinned her nurses badge from her tunic and gave it to me as a memento. I still have it.

At 'The Rehab' I was assessed by the doctors and prosthetists who delivered the disappointing news that the grafted skin on my left stump was too delicate to consider walking on, and it would have to be allowed time to strengthen. I could however begin some physiotherapy. The physios assured me that I would be not only walking, but dancing, by the summer. They asked me to imagine myself dancing again.

That was hard, but I tried. There was, however, an enormous problem. My left knee (the only one I had), was locked straight as a result of the burns, grafting, and lying in bed for months. I couldn't bend it at all, and to use a wheelchair, my left stump was stuck out in front of me, resting on a plank. (My right hand was similarly locked.) The physios explained that in order to walk again, and particularly to go up and down steps, my left knee would have to be bending by at least 90 degrees.

I was told that I must come to the physiotherapy unit everyday at 2pm and that they would bend my knee by an extra one degree every day. A miniature "lagging jacket", made from cotton wool, was devised to protect my grafted stump, and on day one, the 3rd of March, I turned up at the gym. Two physios and an orderly were involved in the procedure. I was helped into sitting on a high table with my stump and locked knee sticking over the edge. One physio produced a giant sized protractor – two wooden rulers joined together by a measuring device, which was put alongside my knee. Whilst the orderly held me down, the other physio began pushing down on my leg until the physio with the protractor announced one degree of bend.

This seemed to me like an awful lot of fuss for just one degree of kneebend, but the physios were insistent that the routine was vital. Indeed, in true Rehabilitation Hospital style, on the few occasions I decided I would prefer to sit in the sun rather than go to physiotherapy, I was tracked down by an orderly and dispatched to the physio with a flea in my ear.

And so, as the days got hotter, the kneebending routine continued and my life in a hospital carried on. I had begun gentle exercising and also spent two hours every day cutting out shapes from sheets of metal in occupational therapy. I was finding that boring but the point, of course, was to force me to use my right hand. I was asked if I played an instrument. I replied that I had played guitar but hadn't had one for years. The next day, a guitar appeared on my bed – which must have been an extra cross for my fellow residents of St. Camillus' Ward to bear. I was introduced to a programme of sports – archery, basketball, pool and table tennis, all played from my wheelchair. I found myself playing table tennis at a competition in Mosney. It felt strange, travelling in the back of a special bus alongside a group of fellow competitors, all with our wheelchairs clamped to the floor of the bus. As a kid I sometimes felt sad whenever I saw a group of disabled or handicapped people in a bus on some type of outing. Sometimes, it was just seeing a face through the bus window, and wondering who that person was, and what their life was like? Now, I was one of the people on the bus. I felt a long way from property deals and nightclubs.

I realised that I was becoming institutionalised in the hospital. There everything was level for your wheelchair. Doors were wide enough and the toilets were easy to use. I felt safe. Although my family home was only five miles away in Bray, and I could have gone home on weekends, I didn't want to. My parents had arranged wheelchair ramps for the steps, and an enormous wheelchair accessible bathroom had been built into the back garden, paid for by The Society of Chartered Surveyors. But I wanted to walk into the house myself. My best pal, Rory Power, was taking me out for drives and trips to McDonalds as much as possible, and was encouraging me to come to his 21st birthday party in June, in the Dungeon Rooms at Killiney Castle. But I knew I wouldn't go in a wheelchair.

One awful incident that contributed to my wanting to stay within the hospital occurred when I was brought back to Dr. Steevens for an out-patient's appointment. I was pushed into a packed waiting room. There was a group of young boys there. As soon as they spotted me their eyes widened with amazement and intrigue. A few of them came over and stood in front of me – just staring at my stumps, not saying a word. It was horrible. I felt like a freak show. Eventually someone moved them out of the room. Another thing I didn't like from that time was that what had always been my "legs" to me, were now referred to by everyone as my "stumps" – which must be one of the most unattractive words in the dictionary. Your left stump. Your right stump.

The days began to pass more quickly as I moved on to weights in the gym and quickly became fitter and stronger. I made friends with lots of the patients, a wide variety of people who by some twist of fate, had found themselves thrown together into this new world. We ate every meal together in the canteen, we worked together, we played sports together and sometimes we cried together. While my injuries were horrific, I soon realised that I had come out lightly in not suffering a brain injury. I certainly felt very lucky compared with the many young people in rows of beds, who were paralysed for the rest of their lives.

I was also struck by the fickleness of fate. I became friendly with one man, in his forties, who was paralysed from the neck down. He could manoeuvre his electric wheelchair around the hospital by moving his chin on a special control pad. He had fallen off a stool in his kitchen trying to change a light bulb.

A beautiful girl in her twenties, formerly a nurse, was paralysed from the waist down. She had fallen backwards as she attempted to climb through a ground floor window after locking herself out of her house. I was beginning to feel lucky. As all of this was going on a good friend of mine crashed his Fiat X19, a small sports car with the roof removed. He lost control on a fast bend, hit a lorry, flipped over a ditch and cartwheeled down a sloping field. I saw the remains of the vehicle later. It was like a scrunched up ball of tinfoil, almost unrecognisable as a car. Luckily, both Conor and his passenger crawled out of the wreckage and miraculously neither required medical treatment. There wasn't a scratch on them! Who knows what forces are at work in these outcomes? Luck? A higher Plan?

We may never know the answer to that question but these thoughts struck me deeply as every day I watched dramatic and unforgettable scenes of people fighting to overcome sudden and drastic changes to their lives. There was a circus performer who had suffered a brain injury, a young English policeman who had suffered a stroke, thalidomide victims with prosthetic arms and legs, and a horrific catalogue of young farmers who had lost limbs in farm machinery. Saddest of all was being with young children who had suffered brain injuries and amputations in accidents, although it was magnificent to see young kids trooping up and down between parallel bars and rapidly adapting to a new way of walking.

My own accident had a few twists of fate too. I had ended up upside-down in a burning car in the middle of the night. It was frustrating to learn, later on, that apparently only 0.25% of cars go on fire after an accident. Had the car not gone on fire, my injuries would have been minor enough. As against that the car was on fire on the forecourt of a petrol station; how the tanks didn't ignite is a miracle. A Mr. Hickmoth, who lived nearby was awoken by the bang. He wasn't sure what the noise had been and at first he checked on his next door neighbour. As he returned to bed, the flames in the distance caught his eye through a window. He grabbed a fire extinguisher from his kitchen (how many houses had fire extinguishers in 1982?) and ran outside. As he reached the crash, the first car to come on the scene, had stopped. It was a taxi. Equipped with a fire extinguisher. By this time, according to my rescuers, I had got myself out, burning, through a window and my saviours used their extinguishers to "put me out".

Incredibly the only two people on the scene, both had fire extinguishers. By another stroke of luck, I was within a quarter of a mile of

Loughlinstown Hospital and I was ambulanced there within minutes, saving my life. So, on the one hand, extraordinarily bad luck but countered by some very lucky twists – without which, I would have burned to death. I remember absolutely nothing of all this – which I suppose is part of the body's defence mechanism.

Another lucky break is that the skin grafting on my left leg runs quite high up the sides of my knee, but dips a couple of inches below my kneecap. On a below knee prosthesis, you take most of your weight on the tendon just under your kneecap and if my grafts had extended over that area too, I would have had even more trouble.

Every admission to the Burns Hospital was announced in the newspapers (generally arising from accidents, fires, explosions and even attempted murder), and it is true to say that the Rehabilitation Hospital has had to face up to its fair share of high profile tragedies.

One dreadful case that is seared into my memory was that of a senior prison officer. An attempt had been made to murder him when he was shot in the back as he left the National Boxing Stadium in Dublin. He survived but was paralysed and was eventually transferred to the National Rehabilitation Hospital. The poor man also seemed unable to communicate. Every day he was wheeled to the gym and was propped up in an enormous brown padded chair. He would be hoisted into a vertical position on the end wall (to drain fluids, I think) and the physios would gently move his limbs. While all of this was going on I was below him, going through my programme of exercises on a floormat. The whole scene struck me as surreal. Whatever about the random accidents that had brought suffering to many of the patients, this man's injuries had been caused deliberately. I felt so sorry for him and shocked at how another human being could have inflicted such suffering on him and his family. As he hung there against the wall, I wondered if he had any idea of what was going on around him or what had happened to him? What on earth did he make of the sight of me – a young man with no legs below him on a mat doing endless sit-ups?

I was very sad but not surprised when I heard the poor man had died.

Extraordinarily, though permeated with tragedy, the atmosphere in the National Rehabilitation Hospital is a happy and uplifting one. The vast majority of patients will leave the hospital in a far better condition than that in which they arrived, equipped and prepared to live their lives to their best potential, albeit doing many things differently, and prepared to face the succession of hurdles and setbacks which go with a disability. There is an amazing camaraderie between patients and staff – a great sense of: "We are all in this together – now let's get on with it."

There was lots of fun and laughter. My ward, the 'prosthetic one' on the top floor, was greatly livened up by the arrival of a man called Mikey. From Kerry he was in his late sixties and had worked all his life with the famous 'Birds' travelling circus. He had lost one leg above the knee but he certainly wasn't going to let it hamper his enjoyment of life. Mikey wore a large multi-coloured floppy hat, which he would inform his audience that he had acquired in the village of Dum Dum, when travelling through India. Every story and fib told to an unsuspecting newcomer was accompanied by a huge wink and a flash of Mikey's tongue as he heaped one unlikely story on another.

Mikey got around quite well by hopping on his one leg and using long wooden crutches under his armpits. He taught me a few of the moves used by the 'three card trick' men and the old fairground 'trick of the loop'. Mikey wasn't too bothered about wearing his new prosthetic leg and it leaned against his bedhead and served as a holder for rolled up newspapers. Many of the patients in the prosthetic ward were elderly men who had suffered amputations due to circulatory problems. Given that many of them had poor hearing and eyesight they made easy prey for Mikey's tricks. One of his favourite routines at about 10pm every night as the ward settled down was to drape a pillowcase over his head, vaguely resembling a nurse or a nun's headgear. He would then hop from bed to bed, holding a notepad and bellow questions at unfortunate patients.

"Did your bowels move?"

"Eh, pardon?"

"Did your bowels move today?" (loud enough for the whole ward to hear)

"Eh, oh yes."

"How many times?"

"Eh, twice, I think."

"Did you take tablets? Which ones did you take?"

The unfortunate victims would then go into a long ramble through their day's activities, with Mikey pretending to take fastidious notes on his pad. This pantomime occurred most nights once the nurses were out of earshot.

On one occasion a busload of patients were taken to Dun Laoghaire harbour to see the departure of a visiting ship from the German Navy. The bus was allowed access to the mouth of the harbour and we were lined up in a row of wheelchairs as the ship approached, very close, and with scores of German sailors lined up on deck, saluting the dignitaries. I often wonder what those sailors made of the line of wheelchairs under the direction of an elderly, one legged man on crutches, who stood proudly to attention whilst giving them a Nazi salute and holding a comb under his nose as a fake Hitler moustache. Oh, and all topped off by a multicoloured hat, from the village of Dum Dum!

Another funny part of hospital life was the manoeuvrings over 'release' from the hospital, into the care of friends. Where medically appropriate, patients could leave the hospital on certain evenings but with a strict curfew. A legendary destination was Bakers Pub about half a mile down the road and curfews were stretched to the limits and all sorts of excuses offered to bristling staff nurses by patients returning late. My own worst example was a night where Rory was permitted to bring me out for two hours.

One thing led to another and we ended up going to some party, and returning at about 2am. The main gates to the hospital were locked. Both inspired and anaesthetised by several pints, we contrived to get the wheelchair over the fence – followed by me, luckily managing to land in it. I then roused a night porter who opened the main door of the hospital. Unfortunately, the lift to my ward on the top floor was out of order, and I had no way of getting up. The porter brought me into the spinal injuries ward on the ground floor where I slipped into a spare bed trying not to wake anyone. As you can imagine, there was a fair bit of controversy the next morning when the day staff came on at 8am, with the prosthetic ward discovering that they had lost a patient, and the spinal injuries ward discovering that they had magically gained a new one overnight. My wings were clipped for a while after that night out.

Throughout this time, work continued on freeing up my hands which were regaining power and the last grafting wounds were healing. There is a driving school attached to the hospital and I was encouraged to learn to drive again, using hand controls. I was nervous initially but I found the new way of driving easy enough to adapt to. Even though I had a full driving licence I had to retake the test on hand controls and after a few lessons with my calm instructor, I passed my test for the second time – which felt like a big step back towards normality and independence.

Just as Christmas had been spent in the burns hospital, my 21st birthday the following May was also spent in hospital. In true "Rehab" fashion, when a crowd of family and friends arrived with six-packs and guitars, beds were pushed back and a right old hooley ensued, with the nurses in great demand for dancing.

By late May I had the plaster casts taken of my two stumps and I had carefully put weight on two rough prototype legs while supported between parallel bars. The prosthetists went off to begin manufacturing my first pair of new legs.

And still the forced kneebending went on.

Some days we got three or four extra degrees quite easily. Other days there was a lot of pain, and a few tears, just to get one extra degree. But we were making progress. And we never stopped. Every day, we got one degree more.

On the afternoon of June 3 the sun was streaming through the windows of a baking gymnasium. That morning I'd taken a few steps on my new legs between bars with the prosthetists. After adjustments the legs were delivered to the gym where the physio would try and take me a little bit further in the afternoon. With frequent stops to check for skin damage I practised up and down between parallel bars. I was doing very well and the physio asked me to try using a walking frame.

Ten minutes later, I was taking my first faltering steps on crutches.

That night I walked down the steep stone steps to the Dungeon Rooms at Killiney Castle for Rory's 21st. It was three months since I first met the physios with their giant protractor. Three months. Ninety days. Ninety degrees. One degree per day.

It was years later before I fully realised what the physios had done. They had given me a goal and a vision and encouraged me to picture it for myself. They had then given me a plan of small steps, (one degree per day), which would see me achieve that goal. And they made sure that I never left out a step. On their own each small step seemed insignificant but put together they quickly added up to something huge. And just like any business there was a team of other people involved, all contributing their own small steps, from prosthetists, to occupational therapists, to doctors. But everyone was sticking to a plan with a timetable. And together they brought a 20-year-old with amputated legs and 76 per cent burns back to working, flying, singing (and dancing).

And my right hand is nearly perfect too – I am using it to write this.

And so I came to realise the power of a programme of small steps and how quickly they can see you achieve a goal which initially seemed almost too much to dare to imagine. I secretly called this my 'Kneebend Principle,'and I began to apply it to achieving goals in both my personal life, and in business.

It never lets me down. And the 'Kneebend Principle' is the bedrock of most of the advice in this book. Establish your goal, work out the steps you need to do differently to get there, never stop doing them and very quickly you will be amazed at what they will add up to.

This principle works very well for organisations who are setting strategic goals or targets for the future. Typically, this involves a day or two's 'think tank', at which senior and middle management brainstorm issues in their business. One unfortunate gets stuck with writing the pages of minutes which he'll struggle to read back at the office. Someone else tries to capture everything on a flipchart with lots of arrows, circles and red and blue markers.

At the end of the 'think tank', a desperate effort is made to prioritise all the ideas and objectives and everyone shoves all their notes into a file. A week or so later a set of minutes goes around with action points for various groups. Three months later very few people can remember what the organisation's No. 1 objective is or who's supposed to be doing what. The next year's annual planning event seems to come around within six months, very little new has been achieved, and the whole process is repeated with renewed determination.

Sound familiar?

Later, I'll show some examples of how to break out of this cycle, but for now, make sure you understand the basic kneebend principle (*see next page*).

Once you start achieving new successes, by sticking to your system you will find that it gets easier to achieve even greater goals. This is because you are moving from being a hopeful participant, to a believer, to ultimately someone who *knows* that their plan will work. Your positive state of mind gives you greater power and your own belief and energy begins to influence those around you who also perform at a higher level.

This is why some individuals and groups in life are seen as hugely successful, as geniuses, as more clever, more effective. They're usually not geniuses but they know what they want, what to do to get it and they don't let anything stop them getting there. Once they are recognised as "successful" or "effective", they get better opportunities and find themselves in better situations. People believe in them and want to be associated with success. They deliver the goods yet again and the success snowball starts. Success breeds success.

More and more I hear people repeat the sayings – "que sera sera/what will be, will be", "C'est la vie/that's life", or "everything happens for a reason" – usually to shrug off something that isn't going their way. The 'reason' is often that they did nothing to make things happen any other way. These are dangerous philosophies in that they acknowledge a 'helplessness' in life which is wrong. We all have the power we need to make changes in our lives and in our businesses.

You can take control.

THE KNEEBEND PRINCIPLE

1. What do I/we want to achieve?

Write it down.

2. By when will I/we have achieved it?

Write down the date

3. What will it be like when I/we have achieved our goal?

Imagine yourself in this new situation. What will you look like? How will my life/business be different? Will I have more money? Imagine what you will be spending it on. Picture that happening. Imagine touching and smelling all the things going on in this new picture. Imagine the taste of champagne as you celebrate. What will people be saying about me/our company?

4. What are the actions I/we need to take, and when?

These are the small steps or the Kneebends, you must take. Write them down. Write down when/how often you need to do them – daily, weekly etc.

5. Stick to it.

Never skip taking a small step. They are all part of the journey.

6. Build in a checkpoint.

More so for a group of people, build in checkpoints, e.g. monthly, to review progress and make sure no-one's out of step. It may be appropriate to make a change, as events unfold.

7. Remind yourself/the group that progress is being made and celebrate notable achievements/milestones along the way.

Keeps you and the group motivated.

8. Celebrate your success in achieving your goal.

Never forget to recognise and reward the behaviours which have brought this new success. Make sure you live out that vision you had at the start – buy that champagne. Think back over the process by which you achieved your goal – it's fun – and reinforces the power and belief you will bring to your next plan.

Of course, having a vision and goals is pretty basic psychology – but it's 'basic' because it's simple. And it works. I'm just another advocate but I'm emphasising the importance of the 'kneebends', the small steps that have to be taken.

I'm particularly suggesting that the 'Kneebend Principle' is vital now when people feel overwhelmed by problems. That's partly because it forces you into breaking everything down and writing a plan. It's much easier to overcome an overwhelming problem by breaking it down into smaller parts to deal with. You're back setting the agenda. You're regaining control. Once you have a plan, you're off to a great start – no more floundering around and firefighting in ever decreasing circles.

The very act of writing a plan with a timetable brings a fresh energy and sense of confidence. In business, it's often the case that "the little things" are overlooked. Often as people prosper up the corporate ladder, it can seem a bit below them to be concerned about the "little things". They get sucked into the world of "management" and start to talk high-level jargon. Issues like the detail of customer service, how your clients regard your telephone answering, the appearance of your premises, handling complaints etc., are all seen as more suited for secretaries, juniors and caretakers.

In fact these are all vital steps on the pathway to success. The "little things" receive scant attention whilst top management wonder why they can't seem to achieve the latest "high level, key strategic objective" to conquer the world. They mean well, the idea is good but they just don't have a system to get there. They've missed identifying all the small steps that need to be taken and they've no system to make sure that they are taken. In corporate life the "kneebend" principle is the most effective method I have seen for getting a group of people to buy into a plan, understand it, implement their own steps and together realise that they've achieved something very big.

In tough times for business such as the present it can be very difficult to keep yourself and people around you motivated. "How many more clients are going to go bust and not pay us? My last three deals have fallen through. There's no chance of a deal here. Every door slams shut. It's hard to see a light at the end of the tunnel." For sure, the days of the "Ra Ra" motivational speaker have gone. You can't just keep blindly trying harder, forever, when nothing seems to be working. What I'm advocating is that the pure exercise itself of breaking everything down into a plan of new small steps will see you become more effective, giving you better results. And to get a change in results, you're probably going to have to change what you're doing.

Here's an example of what I mean. In the estate agency business every now and then we'd get a real problem property – one that seemed destined never to sell. I would usually get to hear about these when a despondent negotiator would come looking for help or when the client began complaining.

A typical example was a Georgian, redbrick house, converted to office use and a doctor's surgery. The property had been on the books for many, many months, but could not be sold. All the client's and negotiator's enthusiasm for each other had evaporated. The price had been reduced and the advertising budget was long spent. The usual brochure had been circulated but very few viewings resulted. Eventually a deal was done but the purchaser could not get finance and pulled out. When another deal was done, the purchaser's surveyor was worried about the roof, so that deal fell through too.

The negotiator was demoralised and just as success snowballs so too can defeat and the negotiator's energy was probably unlikely to convince anyone to buy the building. We quickly thought through a simple plan. The negotiator would write to the client setting out an enthusiastic fresh, low-cost plan.

1. A new upbeat press release was being issued.
2. A press release was being sent to the medical publications.
3. A classified advertisement was being placed for four days.
4. The signboards were being washed.
5. We were printing a leaflet/flyer which the negotiator would put under the windscreen wipers at the car park of the nearby hospital, to target medical professionals.

The property was sold within a fortnight. Now, none of this is genius, and who knows what worked most – the flyer, the press release – perhaps none of them. What I do know is that this chain of events repeated itself so frequently over my 28 years in the property business as to convince me that the breaking down of the problem into small, achievable steps, changed the whole dynamic and the negotiator now believed in a plan which would produce results. His own energy and enthusiasm together with his client's energy and attitude changed and this was needed to achieve a deal.

The negotiator had tried the standard marketing approach, unsuccessfully, over and over. And if you keep doing the same things, you keep getting the same results. So when the going gets really tough, we need a simple plan to change things.

Any of the individual "small steps" in the plan may produce the goods. But I have seen this phenomenon work so consistently over decades that I am convinced that one of the most important factors is in fact the new energy and belief of the negotiator. His new plan is his secret weapon and the new dynamic which he brings to the situation positively influences potential purchasers and his client, and you get a new outcome.

Success!

CHAPTER 2
BACK TO WORK

When I was in the Burns Unit and then the Rehabilitation Hospital for almost a year I was naturally worried about what would become of me. Would I be able to walk properly? Would girls ever go out with me again? A huge worry for me was, would I ever be able to get back to work? In hindsight, I was extremely fortunate on the latter point because my employers, Hamilton Osborne King (now Savills), had a totally positive attitude to my situation from the outset although it must have looked highly unlikely that I could ever return.

But the mere fact that the company was completely committed to helping me return to work was a huge boost for me and kept me going. For a start, the company kept me on full pay while I was out of work which meant that after a year in hospital I could afford to buy a car. Long before I left hospital, Ian French, the Managing Director told me that they had arranged a car parking space for me at the back of the office. When I arrived back into work, unsteady on two crutches, a new computer system had been installed and the company initially suggested that I would look after the computers though I became bored with that after a few hours. This was the mid-1980s and business was tough but I did my best to help out in the commercial departments, trying to get back to where I had been.

On the walking front I had a few tumbles but I had made progress and was by now using only one crutch. I got my first real breakthrough as business began to pick up in our office. A client of ours, Shield Insurance, needed a new office building and Ian French gave me the job of finding it. In fairness to the executives from the insurance company they didn't bat an eyelid when a heavily limping negotiator with a crutch took them in his hand-controlled car on a tour of a number of buildings.

I helped to negotiate a lease of a building in Blackrock – and they're still there. Another breakthrough a little while later came as we got even busier and Aidan O'Hogan asked me to look after the sale of two shop and office buildings in Blackrock's main street. These buildings had many flights of old timber stairs and were harder to get around, but with the physio's voice in my head, "good leg to heaven, bad leg to hell", I managed, and I helped to sell the buildings.

By sticking to my plans of small steps and by setting myself new goals, I gradually got back to the stage of being the same as everyone else at my age level. It was great to be back working routinely selling commercial property. In those days trainees studying Chartered Surveying were directed into handling commercial property only, as distinct from residential, which is a very different business and in fact I never sold a house in 28 years in estate agency.

I no longer needed any crutches and I began to be promoted up through the ranks, to Associate Director and then Director. I was extremely fortunate that Hamilton Osborne King had had such vision, were so positive and gave me every opportunity to re-establish my career. I was very pleased in later years when I was established at senior levels to feel that I was repaying that trust. Twenty years or so later when I was the Managing Director and the firm was acquired by Savills for €50m, Aidan O'Hogan, who had always given me such encouragement, was the lynchpin for that deal, working with his old contact, Jeremy Helsby, the charismatic leader of Savills worldwide. I have had no formal connection with the company for many years but I retain a great appreciation and affection for my first employers, Hamilton Osborne King/Savills and as a company their heart is firmly in the right place.

When I did the Leaving Certificate and left school in 1979 I had just turned 17. I had no real idea of what I wanted to do but I was keen to get working and didn't particularly fancy going to college. I was offered some college places as well as a job in a bank at about £80 per week. Instinctively, I opted for a job as a trainee Surveyor with Osborne King and Megran (later Hamilton Osborne King). My mother had worked for over 30 years as the secretary/receptionist in Southern Estates, a small estate agents in Bray. As kids we would sometimes spend time in that office and I was fascinated by the activity there – people in and out, phones ringing, lots of chatting – it all looked like good fun. So I started out as a trainee surveyor in September 1979 for the grand salary of £1,250 per annum.

Yes, per annum, and without fully realising the implications of doing a Chartered Surveying degree at night by correspondence course. It was a real old apprenticeship system. The system was that the trainee would spend one year working with the late Fintan Lacey, the caretaker, who lived with his family in the top flat of the office building at 32 Molesworth Street. (Molesworth Street played quite a role in my family. Apart from my 28 years there, my mother's first job was in a wine merchants beside the Masonic Hall. And my father proposed to her in a pub where the passport office is now.)

Fintan had a very strong work ethic and was a big influence on me. The whole company revolved around Fintan, who operated from the enormous basement. He made and erected all the 'For Sale' signs, he produced all the brochures, supervised the trainees and ran the building. After a year, depending on Fintan's verdict, you might be promoted up to the daylight of the ground floor and assigned as a junior to some department.

My routine for that year was to get an early train from Bray to Dublin. On the walk to the office I bought maybe 20 bottles of milk and maybe 50 newspapers. On arrival I made the first canteens of tea and coffee and carefully laid out the newspapers on desks. Woe betide the day you left someone an *Irish Times* instead of an *Irish Independent*, or vice versa. From 9 to 11 each morning was spent in the basement where there were 'darkrooms' for photographing the text and photographs for brochures. By 11am you had developed the films and hung them up to dry and we then went out erecting signboards around the city. For every small board to be erected on a garden wall in the sunshine overlooking Killiney Bay, there seemed to be 20 large ones to be erected on the roof of some factory in the freezing, pouring rain. The afternoon was usually spent in the printroom in the basement producing bundles of brochures and sticking photographs on them. At 5.30 I carried a sackful of letters to the post office and some days I would then go back to help Fintan hoover the office. I would get home to Bray about 8pm and then it was supposedly time to study for my Chartered Surveying degree.

Fintan was one of those always busy and cheerful people whom you could ask to do anything and know that it would be done well. After a year I was duly elevated to general dogsbody on the ground floor and now most of my day was spent on the office bike, frantically pedalling around the city with always urgent letters and last minute copy for the newspapers. They were tough enough days but a great learning experience.

I learned a really important lesson from Fintan in that first year on Christmas Eve. The office was open but virtually everyone was down in Buswells Hotel getting into the festive spirit and there were no signs for erection and no brochures to print that day. Fintan being Fintan decided that we would wash the walls in the basement. At about half past three I plucked up the courage to stop and interrupt Fintan, who was washing a wall from the top of a ladder.

"Eh, Fintan."

"Yes, Paul."

"It's half three and everyone's down in Buswells. Is there any chance I can go down, please?"

Fintan briefly stopped scrubbing and peered down at me over the top of his glasses.

"Paul, when you consult your pay packet at the end of the month you'll discover that there was no deduction made for Christmas Eve."

He went back to scrubbing. At about half four, he let me escape. I never got near the work ethic of Fintan Lacey but I never forgot one of his lessons:

"If a job's worth doing, then it's worth doing well."

The year working from the basement produced all sorts of funny stories. One I remember well concerned The Soldiers and Sailors Trust, a charity which provided housing for ex-servicemen. The houses were almost always small cottages and from time to time Fintan and I would be sent out to do some repair or other. One day a routine message came down to the basement – the Managing Director wanted the locks changed on a house off the South Circular Road. We had a signboard to erect in the area so we added this to our jobs for the day.

The house was a redbricked cottage, one of hundreds of identical houses in a series of terraces in Dublin 8. With me navigating we found the house fairly quickly and Fintan forced open the window. We climbed in and began removing the locks in the front door. I remember seeing a bowl of cornflakes and a pint of milk on the table and thinking that the occupiers must have left in a hurry. An hour later, with the locks changed on the front and back doors, we left.

To prevent anyone getting in through the window we had forced, Fintan drove a few nails into the inside window frame. A couple of weeks later a message came down to us enquiring as to when we were going to change the locks at the Soldiers and Sailors house. We advised that we had already done it. A couple of days later "upstairs" was insisting the job wasn't done. It turned out that we had been in the wrong house. At that stage we no longer had the address we had used and we couldn't remember what house we had been at. I often wonder if the occupiers ever figured out what had happened after returning home to find their locks changed and the windows nailed up.

The long period as a bicycle messenger boy was also hectic but good fun. There was the twice daily trips to the Document Exchange, a daily visit to the Bank with various lodgements, the mad dashes to the newspapers and the daily bun-run to Fuscos with a long order book of cakes and buns for the staff. I enjoyed charging around the city centre and I got to know all sorts of characters including various messenger boys for the offices in the area and all of the bank and hotel porters. An interesting treat every now and then was to be designated as a porter when the firm was handling a clearance sale in a big house. There was always great fun at these. I remember being a porter at the clearance auction at 90 Merrion Square – at the time it was the last private residence on the Square. Days spent carrying furniture down staircases were hard work but you would earn more in a day in tips than from your week's salary.

The early years spent as a junior in the commercial department provided excellent experience. I was still the general dogs-body and delivery boy but I now had a desk. I would also be taken out on inspections and was assisting in measuring buildings, handling telephone enquiries and viewings. I love a good practical joke and we had great fun playing jokes on each other – and on our peers in the other firms of auctioneers.

When President Ronald Reagan visited Dublin in 1984, there was to be an open-top cavalcade through the city centre. A week or so before his arrival, calling myself John Hinckley and doing a poor attempt at an American accent, I called my contemporaries in the other firms, pretending I was looking for offices to rent – short term.

Unusually, I wanted the offices to be as high up in the building as possible. When they asked about my ideal location, I read out the route map for the presidential cavalcade. A couple of people arranged appointments with Mr. Hinckley but he never showed up. In the realm of our practical jokes anyone who didn't remember that John Hinckley had shot and injured Ronald Reagan in 1981 and fell for that enquiry was fair game.

Another ongoing prank involved a blue Ford Anglia – just like the Harry Potter one, which had been sold on, year after year in the firm from one junior to another and was now owned by Liam Lenehan. It was a bit of a banger but a headturner, even in the early eighties. I had managed to secretly make a copy of the keys and one day I parked the Anglia in the managing director's space in the garage, which caused a fair old fuss. Over a period of months, when the Anglia owner was out, I would turn the Anglia around in its car space, then changed to moving it a few spaces down the road, and then across the street. After a few months, Liam would be routinely walking around the block, looking for his car.

Throughout all of this, I would swear innocence and point at the previous owners as the prime suspects – as they must have kept a set of keys. Inevitably, it came to pass that the Anglia owner scored a major revenge prank on me. As part of a truce, we held a light-hearted returning of the keys ceremony and we pricked our fingers and swore in blood that we would never talk about the matter further. That lasted until the next Friday night in the pub. Another memorable one was when I was measuring up a garage which had closed and there were dozens of old car number plates strewn around. Thinking that they would have to come in handy sometime, I took an armful back to base and using elastic bands coloured black, I changed the number plates on a number of colleagues cars and a few of the "oppositions."

A number of funny stories developed from that, the best of which was the arrest of a leading auctioneer who was taken to Pearse Street Garda station to explain why there were different numbers at either end of his MG. And they were both wrong. In hindsight, this may not have been the most admirable behaviour and you certainly had to keep your wits about you in those days in Dublin 2.

As I moved up through the ranks and gained experience, I met all sorts of interesting people, clients, purchasers and tenants. I rented a studio to the artist Cecil King. We got on well and had a few laughs. When I asked him for a trade reference he grandiosely wrote out a note, put in an envelope and handed it to me. When I opened it later it simply read:

"Trade Reference – The Pope, The Vatican, Rome, Italy. (I recently did his head.)"

I did a lot of work in the Dublin docklands long before it was anything but a very tough, semi-derelict area. I did a few deals with Harry Crosbie and we got on very well to the extent that I did almost all of his commercial work. When he needed me to look at something he would say that he was sending "the singing auctioneer."

One day in the mid-eighties Harry called me and asked was I free as he needed my advice on something. He picked me up and took me down to a massive old CIE train shed in the docks called The Point Depot. We stood in the middle of the shed beside trains at a siding. Harry asked what did I think of it as a concert venue?

I was completely taken aback. It's hard now to try to explain what the docks were like back then – parts of it were a no-go area and the idea of trying to run concerts there seemed mad. As an example of how tough it was, a while earlier Harry had moved containers into a yard on North Wall Quay, where the Convention Centre is now. On the first day he was threatened with dire consequences unless he paid protection money. Harry refused and engaged a security company with instructions to put their two fiercest dogs into the yard that night. The following morning, the two Alsatians had been decapitated and their heads were impaled on stakes in the middle of the yard. This was a quarter of a mile from where Harry wanted to put on concerts.

I told him that I couldn't really see the vision, but he wasn't for stopping and I acted for him in buying the property at tender. These days it's the magnificent O2 arena, surrounded by apartments, hotels, offices and retailing, with a train station and great access, and it all looks so obvious. I admire Harry and others like him, for their vision – and for staking their money on that vision, when everyone else thinks they're crazy.

Another very interesting day was spent with Sir Anthony O'Reilly in the lead car of a convoy of limousines as we chose the site for Independent Newspapers new printing headquarters at Citywest. After we met, he immediately tested me out with a few questions on politics and planning tribunals. The morning passed quietly enough but once our work was accomplished, the last hour or so was a highly entertaining discussion on world affairs, liberally sprinkled with his sharp impersonations of various world leaders.

Over the years, I developed a great interest in the masterplanning of large commercial sites and I still get a buzz of satisfaction when I pass some of the schemes in which I was involved, from the docklands to business park schemes like Westgate Business Park where I located TV3, to Fashion City to the The Park, Carrickmines.

Throughout all of these years of steady progress, I never forgot my 'Kneebend Principle' to keep me going and to make sure I completed projects and didn't just talk about them. You can make my 'Kneebend' system work for you. Don't be afraid to 'think big' when setting your goal, but it might be better not to attempt to dominate your market and buy your competitors straightaway.

Pick a new objective, something that you would really value achieving, but which, in truth, you know is not going to happen unless you really change your behaviour. Remember, in the business world six months will go by in the blink of any eye. Yet in six months your company can have achieved a notable advance in your marketplace if you start implementing a 'kneebend' system now. When you have become better and better at working the system, and you are looking back at some big achievements, you can set your sights even higher. You will realise that you now have the power and the system to achieve anything you want.

When you sit down to write a plan of small steps for your new objectives you must think hard and in simple terms about what steps you need to take – they're probably staring you in the face. It is always worthwhile asking somebody smart for an outside view. As I work with successful companies, often attending strategy meetings and board meetings, I am constantly surprised at how often groups of people can miss obvious solutions. What happens is that they become too close to the problem, analyse it to death and end up missing the obvious. The old phrase applies: "Sometimes we can't see the wood for the trees."

What you will be doing now is stringing those important new steps together properly for the first time. Before you know it they will have added up to something huge. And exciting. Later on, I'll show how the 'Kneebend Principle' can be used to transform your Customer Service. For another example of how the system works, see Chapter Eleven, "The Weapons of Mass Instruction".

In the following chapters, I have laid out my views on some of the most important areas for success in business. They are areas where you can achieve real improvements and see real benefits, at very little cost. No matter what new goals you are setting for yourself or your business, these following chapters can all probably be regarded as 'small steps' or 'the little things', which may or may not form part of your plan.

No matter how you prioritise them, by paying a little new attention to some of these issues, you will definitely find that you will become outstanding and your business will be regarded as much stronger within months. At the heart of everything I urge you to work hard at deepening your understanding of the crucial importance of customer service. But all business involves people and how they interact. So let's talk about birds...

// CHAPTER 3 //
CANARIES, ROBINS AND DODOS - LET'S GET BLUNT!

How good your customer service is depends on how good your people are. The right training will pay for itself over and over again. But I'll save you money by telling you that there's little point in training about 15 per cent of your staff. Here's why:

Have you ever come across someone in an office, a shop, hotel or on the telephone where you instantly know that you are in the hands of an expert? Where you just know that you are going to get the very best service and attention? From your first interaction with them they are friendly, smiling, enthusiastic about helping you and they know their job inside out. If the interaction started with a complaint or a problem they seem naturally to understand your point of view. You instantly realise that if anything goes wrong you can really trust this person, they're taking this personally. Not only that but they're enjoyable to deal with – even fun to deal with. And they seem to enjoy helping you. They only have sensible and positive suggestions – nothing is a problem. You look forward to dealing with them again. You wish there was a few more people like this in the other places you deal with in your life. Congratulations, you've just met a "Canary".

Canaries don't need any training in customer service, they're naturals, they instinctively know what to do and they'll always get it right. They are emotionally intelligent, enthusiastic, keen to get on, instinctively good with people, confident, fun, reliable and hardworking, with a can-do attitude. People like dealing with them and working with them. They cheer you up. They are bright, chirpy, quick and colourful – that's why I call them Canaries. Put a Canary in any situation and they'll do the right thing. But, they are a maximum of five per cent of the people you'll meet in business. Canaries generally rise pretty quickly to the top of organisations or if their wings are clipped by low standards around them, they'll quickly move on and rise to the top somewhere else. Canaries are gold dust. Seek them out and put them in key positions.

My cousin, Alan Stoner, left Ireland in the 1950s aged 17, with a £20 note in his pocket. He was headed for McAllen, Texas, close to the border with Mexico where he had a job lined up as a trainee manager, sweeping the floor at a small restaurant called "Whataburger".

Now Alan flies back to Ireland on a Lear Jet to play golf. He recently 'retired' as senior vice-president at Whataburger. They have grown to over 1,250 restaurants and are the biggest restaurant chain in the South-East region. Alan says that he built that empire on 'Canaries' – always finding the right person to run a restaurant, to manage regions, to do the property deals. Alan owns a number of restaurants himself and travels the US as a speaker on customer service in the hospitality sector and serves on various boards. Alan's a Canary himself.

At the National Rehabilitation Hospital in 1983 I was lucky enough to meet another Canary called Kevin Carroll who was a prosthetist there. To gain experience he was seconded to a prosthetics company in Oklahoma. He returned full of new ideas and fortunately for me, together with the late Jimmy McKenzie, outside of normal working hours he experimented in trying new types of limb-fitting techniques – and improved my walking and comfort.

He helped introduce the latest technology into the hospital. Of course Kevin had made a big impact too in the US and was offered a senior position there and he took the gamble of moving his young family to Oklahoma. Twenty five years later, he is vice president of the Hanger Corporation, personally responsible for 175 clinics in the US. When the UK government asked the US authorities for help in looking after amputee soldiers returning from Iraq and Afghanistan, the US government sent Kevin Carroll from Tipperary. After the Haiti earthquake Kevin brought a team there and has fitted hundreds of survivors with prosthetic limbs. He achieved further fame recently when he succeeded in fitting 'Winter', an injured dolphin in Florida with a prosthetic tail.

The technology developed in that process is now being used to help humans with damaged skin. Hollywood heard the story and made the blockbuster film 'Winters Tale' with Morgan Freeman playing the part of Kevin Carroll, the prosthetist. Kevin spends every week travelling around clinics solving limb-fitting problems, returning to his family in Orlando at weekends. He regards nothing he does as work. As a typical Canary trait, he has a large collection of classic and antique stringed instruments – guitars, bangos, mandolins, ukuleles etc – all of which he plays to a professional standard. Kevin has all the characteristics of a Canary in abundance – a totally positive, "can-do" attitude, an enthusiasm for life and people, a constant quest for knowledge and new challenges as well a strong work ethic.

There's another Canary I met called Jimmy O'Shea, who owns James Herren Menswear on Dawson Street. As soon as you go into the shop you get great natural attention, smiles, banter about sport and good fun. Years ago I went in and the background music was The Brotherhood of Man which I teased them about. Now when I go in there's a scramble to put on the Brotherhood of Man tape. Jimmy's staff follow his lead. He'll always give you a few euro off your bill. (I'm sure most people get this, but it makes you feel good).

I worked around the corner for years and anytime you needed a clean shirt, Jimmy would have it ironed and delivered to you. If you forgot your cufflinks, Jimmy had an emergency selection which he'd deliver to you. He doesn't charge you for alterations and never lets you buy anything if he's not 100 per cent happy that it's perfect for you. One day I was standing at the doorway of James Herren chatting to Jimmy. It was raining. Suddenly Jimmy said, "Excuse me, Paul." He ducked into the shop, grabbed an umbrella and ran off down the street. When he came back he explained that he had spotted a customer walking down the other side of the street wearing one of his suits, and he didn't want to see him getting it wet. That's Canary behaviour. That's why James Herren is there for 20 years while many other menswear shops have opened and closed all around him.

Those are just a few of the Canaries I've met so far. My mother was another. Canaries will always exceed normal expectations and even without academic qualifications have the ability to take on any task and do it well. You can find Canaries passing through all levels of life and business. They're rare but they'll stand out a mile. So treasure them – they are gold dust.

At the bottom of the pile in every business including your business is the weakest 10 per cent, the lowest performing group. They are spread across all areas and some of them are in senior positions. To save us time I'm going to call them the Dodos. I sincerely hope that you haven't got any Dodos in positions where they have to deal with your clients because they are doing you a lot of damage. I see Dodos almost every day and there are lots of them in customer facing jobs who should not be there. Dodos are the opposite of Canaries. You can usually spot them out in the wild from a distance of about 50 feet from their body language and expression. Slouching, backs turned to customers, sullen expressions and poor presentation are all signs of a Dodo. They are not particularly good with people and they show very little enthusiasm for anything. They can sometimes be hardworking but they have no initiative.

Their attitude is negative, they come up with problems but no ways around them. They see their job as just doing the basics, covering their ass and will never look for an opportunity to 'go the extra yard' with a client or colleague. From a customer service point of view they are brain-dead and colleagues hate working with them too.

Dodos.

That is not to say that they are not intelligent, decent, nice, honest people – they probably are. They just should never be operating in a competitive environment and dealing with your customers, on your payroll. And definitely never in reception (but some are). If your trainer is honest he will say that you will be wasting your money in trying to train the Dodos – you will get very little response for your money. The Dodos just haven't got it. It's genetic. You must eliminate Dodos from your organisation because they have a negative effect on colleagues and they will make your business extinct.

By the way, the Dodo group will usually include the character described by the great motivational speaker, Watt Nicoll, as 'the Black Abbott'. Every organisation has one – and they're often pretty senior.

I call this character "The Raven" – the classic harbinger of doom. The

Raven sees his job as being "to protect our right to be as miserable as we like here, for as long as we like." One of his most common phrases is: "That'll never work here." The Raven is a negative influence in most businesses and will block change at every opportunity because he/she believes that they know the best way to do things. They feel threatened by change.

As a general rule you should be constantly weeding the Dodos out and always trying to replace them with better people because they will block progress in your business. The Raven though is usually the most difficult to remove. Normally, with their experience and longevity, they've worked out how to cover their ass, they have a few medals from old battles, credibility with a few clients and they're well organised and good at politics. Remove or sideline the Raven as soon as possible.

Which brings us to the Robins – which includes most of us. That is the 85 per cent grouping of staff in your business, who are "in the middle". This is the group that you should be focusing on because this is the group that can and will respond to training, to new ideas and encouragement. This is where you get the best return on your training and effort because most of this group can and want to up their performance. They just need to be shown the way, encouraged and rewarded. I call this group the Robins.

In the wild, we see more Robins than Canaries. Robins aren't as colourful as Canaries but they're likable, intelligent, quick and chirpy. Robins are mostly brown but they have that beautiful colourful bright red breast – and that's what we're encouraging our Robins to show us more of, their best side, their most colourful and attractive display, and more often. With the right guidance and encouragement many Robins can operate for long periods at the same level as Canaries – and that's our goal. We want them to bring more colour into their job.

Lastly, another story which emphasises that it's not all that difficult to switch your staff into enjoying upping their attention to customers and strategically moving a company to being outstanding. About 18 months ago I was contacted by Martin Carway, the managing director of a firm of loss adjustors called ProAdjust, located near Dublin's Naas Road. They are a leading firm in their sector with about 45 staff and they handle thousands of claims annually for major insurance companies. Martin explained that he wanted to improve the standard of their customer service. He pushed a pile of documents across the desk at me. "Have a read of that," he said. It was one of the most comprehensive and detailed 'mystery shopping' surveys I have ever seen with reports and scores going back years.

Martin explained that one of his biggest clients, a multinational insurance company, mystery shopped all of the brokers working on its behalf – and mystery shopped the insurance company's own staff. Also, another insurance company client had called him in and expressed concern at the level of complaints being generated. I read the 'mystery shopping' reports. As I usually find, most of the brokers were tightly grouped around the same score with the odd exception under a couple of headings. Martin's concern was that ProAdjust were firmly stuck at an average ranking for several years and he wanted to be better than average. He invited me to speak to his team on an annual day away from the office – which was partly to celebrate a great year – and part training.

A few weeks later I found myself standing in front of ProAdjust's 45 staff in a Dublin hotel. I had an hour, from 2-3pm. They were enthusiastic and responsive. Firstly we discovered, as is often the case, that there was no common view at all in the room as to which broker provided the best service. This reflected the 'mystery shopping' – in fact everyone was very similar. We then talked about how (as is often the case with brokers and agents) they actually have two customers for every job. One is their client, the insurance company. But the policyholder, who is making the claim, is a customer too. Because if the policyholder does not feel good about how he was treated during the claim, he will take his business elsewhere.

We then had some good fun talking about Canaries, Robins and Dodos; we touched on examples of 'Canary Alerts' that occurred in their daily work and how everyone was responsible for making their client feel special.

We also spent a few minutes chatting about dealing with complaints and most importantly, sorting out problems at source before they became a complaint.

Over the following year or so I kept in touch with Martin and was pleased to hear that "Canaries, Robins and Dodos" had become part of the vernacular at ProAdjust. Just days before this book went to print I received a phone call from a very happy Mr. Carway. He had just received the annual 'mystery shopping' survey from his client. ProAdjust had "romped home" as the winner in all categories. They had also scored higher than the insurance companies' own staff. Their client was delighted with them. I was delighted too. A great example of how a little extra attention to customer service at no great cost can move a company's service from average to outstanding. ProAdjust agreed to let me tell this story of their experience.

The way forward is clear – turn Robins into Canaries and send your Dodos into extinction.

//CHAPTER 4//
CUSTOMER SERVICE - MAKE 'EM FEEL SPECIAL

"Customer Service". Two simple words. A simple concept. Thousands of books and training sessions have set out to improve a business's customer service. Everyone agrees that it is important, and seems to understand it. Yet, so few people really get it.

So few businesses really get it.

Almost every company will say that they regard customer service as a key objective or value – but there's very little evidence of this on the ground. Usually they get away with it because most of their competitors have settled for the same standard. Every time I talk to business people, whether in a social or business setting, everyone enthusiastically agrees that 'customer service' is a top priority. And everyone loves telling their favourite stories about very good and very bad service that they encountered. Yet these people often can't see poor customer service and bad habits all around them in their own companies. There is an assumption, particularly in professional services companies, that not only are we providing a very good service but it is probably better than the average of our competitors. Many large organisations in the business of providing a service will have department heads for all sorts of functions – but not for 'customer service.' There's an assumption that they are good at that. Every few years they'll get someone in to talk about customer service but it is not treated as a core value.

As a general rule the more a company grows the worse its customer service gets. This is because it becomes difficult to make sure that every staff member really understands the importance of "Make 'em feel special". To cope with the sheer numbers of staff, procedures manuals are written to try and explain to the employee what to do in certain situations. And that's a poor form of communication. The message isn't 'sticky' enough and the impact dilutes over time. In fact it's usually in the situations where things go wrong, when the unexpected scenario arises that you really need your staff member trained and empowered to be creative and to use their personality in making that customer feel special – no matter what. Unless you have totally committed customer service advocates placed in the right areas and leading by example every day, it is difficult to maintain a very high standard and the customers will experience wide variations in service from the same company.

Another big problem I see in large companies is that recognising the importance of customer service, they create 'Customer Care Channels' and 'Customer Service Departments' where they put some good people to cover customer care and complaints. The problem is that this becomes a culture and deflects the focus on customer service away from the frontline staff in the sales or service departments, who in fact are winning and losing business all day, depending on how they are dealing with customers. And those frontline departments can become overly focused on achieving sales targets etc, because they report to a sales director and 'customer service' belongs to another department. Very dangerous.

The huge opportunity in business is to realise that you only have to improve your customer service a notch or two to be outstanding in your sector. I was never great at maths but by definition, *most* of the competitors in a sector provide *average* service. View it from a customer's or client's point of view. Take a look at the main players in any business sector – lawyers, accountants, car dealers, retailers, hoteliers, manufacturers. Look at their websites – they generally all look the same, and say the same things. They'll all espouse customer service as a "value". They'll all have a similar offering in terms of services, departments, products, spread of offices, and overseas networks etc. They'll have broadly similar numbers of employees. Their employees will have similar qualifications, experience and personalities. And guess what? They'll all provide a similar quality of customer service.

And that's the opportunity.

This phenomenon is reinforced for me every time I work with a client company. Any available information, from surveys, questionnaires, client ratings or mystery shopping scores inevitably show all the main players grouped tightly together around a similar score. Which means if the average quality of customer service is say 7 out of 10, all you have to do is 'tweak the dial' to get your own standard to 8.5 or 9 to be outstanding. You don't have to double the quality of your service or try and change the world. Just tweak the dial – and keep it tweaked.

Everybody has heard by now that if you provide a customer with a better quality of service than they *expected* they'll come back and give you more business. If you really made a big impact with your service they'll tell lots of people how good you are. And those people will become customers too. That's the best way to grow a business. The challenge with 'customer service', for any business, is to find a way that inspires every person in the company to understand that their own individual actions, dozens of times every day, are either winning or losing business. Inspiring in such a way that the value of providing an outstanding level of customer service becomes part of the culture and lasts a lot longer than the two week wonder you usually get after a staff training session before everyone goes back to their old ways.

I am 100 per cent convinced that the best way for any business to thrive and prosper in the long term is by providing a better standard of customer service than your competitors. If you think about it 'customer service' is really the only strategy guaranteed to set you apart. Look at the alternative strategies: For example, to gain market share you could decide to lower your fees or prices. Yet if this proves successful, your competitors will quickly do the same. You might decide to invest in expensive cutting-edge technology which will bring you big efficiencies and lower costs. Again, if you are right, your competitors will quickly do the same. You might decide to open a new department providing a new type of service. If it was a good idea your competitors will copy you and any advantage will soon be lost. But if you successfully put a plan in place to raise your permanent standard of customer/client service above your competitors they can't react!

For a start they won't know what you've done. Lots of little things about your company will be better but they won't be able to spot the strategy. They will however, spot that you seem to be winning more business than you used to. Even when they eventually hear that you have adopted a strategy to 'out-service' them, they may not be able to react at all. Or certainly not in the short term. Because having superior customer service in a company, having a passion for customer service, is a cultural thing. You can't write a cheque and buy it. You can't announce to the staff that you are all going to be providing a new higher level of customer service next year and expect anything to change. An organisation needs as many passionate advocates for customer service as possible who lead by example and the more at senior level the better. If your competitor doesn't have a passionate activist for better customer service, who's prepared to live or die for the cause, then "they ain't gonna get there".

In business, I will happily admit to a passion for customer service. Some people would call it an obsession. Everyday as I interact with businesses I find myself sub-consciously rating everything they do – from the appearance of their premises, to the greeting in reception, to signage, telephone answering, advertising, and the quality of the people you meet. I would like to think that I successfully reinforced and lived a culture of outstanding customer service at the estate agency I was with for almost 30 years. Remember a business could go bust whilst providing the highest level of customer service in its sector, for example, by overstaffing, giving away misguided discounts, gifts, and a loose attitude of solving customer issues by throwing money at them. Yet, and here's the joy of it – providing the outstanding level of customer service in your market, is FREE. Or costs very little.

Here's How To Do It:

First off, remind yourself of some examples of why customers and clients come back for more of your business. Think of some recent examples of good and bad customer service which you experienced and which will determine whether or not you give that company any more of your business. Here's two favourites of mine:

GREAT CUSTOMER SERVICE

Often when in Dublin city centre I call my old firm and see if any of my old colleagues are free at lunchtime for a sandwich. I usually go to the

Bailey, a well known pub/restaurant, just one of dozens nearby. My pal, Mark Reynolds, asked me recently, "Why do you always go to the Bailey?"

I said, "It's because of the customer service."

I told him how a few months before I had gone into the Bailey and sat down. I was thirsty and decided I wanted a Lucozade with my sandwich. A Chinese waitress came to take my order. She gave me a nice smile. I asked her if they had Lucozade.

She said, "Sorry, no, but we have Coke or 7up...? Or sparkling water?

"Hmmm – no," I said. I must have looked disappointed.

"Don't worry," she said with a smile, "I'll get you Lucozade." She walked behind the bar and picked up a bottle of Coke. She walked out the door of the Bailey and across the street to a pub called Davy Byrnes. Thirty seconds later she was back at my table pouring my Lucozade. She had swopped her Coke for my Lucozade.

Brilliant.

Simple.

Costs nothing.

Because of this gem of customer service, a group of my friends have regularly eaten lunch there. I suspect she worked the system out for herself and the staff were not trained or instructed to do this.

More recently I was there and repeated the request for a Lucozade. A different waitress couldn't think beyond offering Coke or 7up. So I had tap water. That Chinese waitress is a Canary, but even though she has long gone, I still go back. Which shows you the power loyalty and memory attaching to a simple yet outstanding customer service. Can you harness this power into your business?

BAD CUSTOMER SERVICE

Regularly I received from a leading luxury motor main dealer a glossy leaflet inviting me to play golf on their "client corporate day". I have been buying new cars from that manufacturer since 1988. In 1999, I went to one of their dealerships in Dublin and bought a brand new car. It had lots of little extras, and I even booked a special registration number. The salesman was very good. The car was getting rave reviews and almost jokingly I asked him if there was anything about the car that wasn't perfect. He said that the only thing they had noticed was that the CD changer unit in the boot was causing problems for some customers.

The new car was superb. After nine months or so, the CD changer got stuck on the Robbie Williams song 'Angels'. I was busy and it wasn't enough of a reason to bring the car back to the dealer. Six months later I knew every word and every note of 'Angels' and the car was due a service. I brought the car in and wrote down the usual list of small things to be attended to, including the faulty CD changer. When I collected the car that evening I paid an expensive bill and turned on the ignition – to instantly hear the familiar sound of 'Angels'. The serviceman (let's call him Tom) explained that everything had been done except the CD changer which was "out of warranty".

I wasn't too happy so I asked to see the service manager, (let's call him Dick). Dick explained that they had made a call to (let's call him Harry) at the car importers head office, requesting that they authorise a repair (in other words, pay for it), as a goodwill gesture. Harry hadn't been available, so Dick told me that he would be in touch shortly. I never heard from them again. I continued listening to 'Angels' for another year or so and every time it came on I thought angrily about my motor dealership.

As a revenge for how they had treated me, and for making me allergic to Robbie Williams, I decided not to buy another one of their cars. The next time I bought a car I changed to another make because of how I felt about my own dealer. Another two years later I went back to my favourite make for a new car but this time I drove past my nearby dealer and bought the car from a dealer on the other side of the city. And three other new cars since. (They collect and deliver your car for servicing). And still I continued to get brochures and invitations to play golf from my original dealer who doesn't even know that they have lost a customer.

Or why.

That company and staff completely lost touch with me as a customer. Interestingly I was telling this story to someone recently and they laughed as it struck a chord with them. A few years ago when business was very good, this man had treated himself to his dream car – a second-hand version from his local dealer. He loved that car. The following winter he spun on black ice and crashed heavily. The car was badly damaged but not quite a write-off. He left the car with his dealer who also did body repairs. When he collected it he was delighted with the job but soon discovered that all 16 CDs were missing from the changer in the boot. He raised this with the manager who said he would investigate and get back to him but never did.

They were his favourite 16 CDs. He listed them off. Pink Floyd – 'Dark side of the Moon', Van Morrison etc. Even if one of the dealers staff had stolen them the dealer could have replaced them for maybe €200 – out of a repair bill of many thousands for a good customer. But the manager didn't bother – he couldn't see the emotional value of this to his customer. My friend bought his next car from another dealer and will never go back to his local dealer whom he feels abused him. This type of thing goes on all the time in business.

Could there possibly be any Tom, Dick or Harrys in your organisation who don't have the intuition, training or authority to do the right thing for your clients? They are losing you business every day.

LEVERAGING CUSTOMER SERVICE

It's good to remind ourselves of the powerful impact of good and bad customer service – the small actions of individuals – and how much business it can win for you and how many clients you can turn away for ever.

The concept of 'leveraging' has negative connotations from the meltdown in the financial markets. But 'leveraging' can have a very powerful, positive effect for your company if you can get everyone to improve their customer service by just 10 per cent. It would be difficult for you to drastically change the quality of service your company provides on your own (especially if your colleagues are not helping). But if everyone ups their game by 10 per cent, all of these improvements add up to a much bigger improvement. Most of your competitors are providing a similar standard of service – you just need to get a little bit ahead to be outstanding and to become the winner.

As in sport, the margins between business competitors are usually very small. The differences between success and failure, winning or losing that job, are often tiny. The power of leveraging is that extra strength you can bring to your organisation. Get everyone to understand that just 10 per cent more effort with customers, just one more goal each this year is the difference for your company between average and outstanding.

In the Olympic games just hundredths of a second will separate a number of finalists in some events. Following Derval O'Rourke's last European hurdling final, I heard the commentator remark that all the finalists, from first to last, had finished within the same second and all within one metre on the track.

So the margins between The Best and The Worst are often small – and the same applies in business. Your opportunity is to be that little bit better, to have all of your team trying that little bit harder at every little step. That's the way to become outstanding.

A final thought on leveraging. Most of the business owners/managers I work with readily accept that they are working at close to maximum capacity already, working too many hours in the week. If you can't work any harder how can you create more value, more profit? The answer is that you must have something else working for you – and that is your brand, the powerful word of mouth that informs the market that you provide the best service. This brings you more and more customers.

Leveraging. By simply showing your staff and empowering them to use their intuition to give customers/clients a better experience, they will begin winning new customers all day every day and adding far more than anyone can by working an extra ten hours a week.

Leveraging!

Imagine how powerful an effect it would be on your business if you had all your staff taking the actions equal to the Chinese waitress at every opportunity rather than the car dealer's men who couldn't see what to do. By creating a culture of outstanding customer service in your company, by making it clear to everyone that you hold customer service as a core value of the company, by recognising and rewarding outstanding customer service by your staff, and by consistently leading by example, you can create a powerful snowballing effect of outstanding customer service, which your customers and clients will love and your competitors will envy.

MAKE 'EM FEEL SPECIAL

In 2004, I was asked to step up to the position of managing director in Hamilton Osborne King, a market leading firm with about 200 staff. Wisely, my predecessor recommended that I continue the company tradition for new managing directors of attending a course on leadership at the London Business School. This turned out to be a seven day, 9am to 10pm, very intensive programme, attended by about 60 people from organisations all over the world. Most of them were due to be promoted to leadership positions. It was fantastic.

I strongly recommend anyone at senior management level to undertake something similar – you will have far more insight and be better prepared for the task. Some of my learning from that course is laced through this book. There was a lot of teaching on communication and it was impressed on the students how important our inaugural speech as leader would be, in that everyone in your organisation would be interested in, or anxious about new plans or changes for the company. You would, in effect, be setting out your stall.

In my case a function was planned for a Friday evening in the head office and all staff were invited in to hear the new managing director announced. I had plenty of time to think about this and I set out to write the barnbuster speech of all time. Drawing on all my new knowledge on communication, I ended up writing two speeches.

Speech One was the Nelson Mandela version in that it opened with one of his quotations while speech two was the JFK blueprint. I had struggled between the need to be inspiring and saying something concrete yet obviously, with all staff there, including transient graduates, there's only so much you can say about company strategy or change.

Both speeches were well rehearsed but by 3pm on the day I still wasn't entirely happy with either and couldn't decide which to go with. With the pressure mounting, I told my secretary that I needed to get out of the office to think and I found a quiet seat in the corner of Buswells Hotel, opposite Dail Eireann, where I had an epiphany.

I noticed an old man shuffling his way into the lobby. He was bent over, almost double, and using a stylish brown walking cane with a polished brass top. He was beautifully dressed. He was wearing a crisp navy suit, a white shirt and a yellow tie, with small black spots, complemented by a yellow and black spotted silk pocket handkerchief.

He wore an enormous, old style, gold pocket watch on his waistcoat. Topping all this was a black hat with a natty yellow feather. He was well into his eighties. He slowly reversed towards an armchair and started to lower himself carefully down but seemed to get stuck halfway to the chair. I jumped up to help by taking a little of his weight and lowered him down. He looked up at me and said, "thank you" and I suddenly realised who it was.

It was Mr. McGuire.

The same Mr. McGuire who had given me my greatest ever lesson in customer service at a crucial point in my career. He asked how I was getting on and showed genuine delight when I told him I was about to be announced as the new managing director. I reminded him of the lesson he had given me 20 years earlier and thanked him for his insights.

The story goes like this: In 1982, I was an up and coming 20-year-old negotiator in the commercial department of the estate agents. But recession was biting, some people had been let go and I found myself as the junior in a merged Offices and Investments Department, with a large portfolio of properties to sell and no-one with any interest or money to buy them. One such property was a large commercial investment property in Blackrock, Co. Dublin, let out as offices, storage units, workshops and some apartments. (One garage was let to the Red Cross and a bizarre sight was to open the door to find it piled high with second-hand artificial legs.)

Mr. McGuire was the vendor, our client. Full of enthusiasm and helpfully not really knowing what a recession meant I started ringing through old lists of enquirers. I found someone who would view the property and I eventually ended up negotiating a sale at about £400,000 (which was a lot of money in 1982). I was the 'fair haired boy' in the commercial department. I earned a nice commission, and the company was delighted with the fee.

By 1985, the recession was deepening and property deals were almost impossible. One Wednesday the newspaper property supplement announced that a particular commercial property investment had been sold for about £250,000. I got a sick feeling in my stomach when the article told me that the purchaser was Mr. McGuire, who had been advised by another agent. Which meant that another agent had earned a big fee.

I felt a bit let down. "But this was my client! I did a good job for him – how could he not use me?" Curiosity got the better of me and I rang Mr. McGuire and arranged to see him at his office. He knew what was on my mind. We got to it pretty quickly. I expressed disappointment that he had changed agents and hadn't told me he was in the market for another property. There was a pause. He was a small man, in his sixties at that time, and he leaned back, choosing his words.

"Paul, you and your company never made me feel special. I was a big client, did one of the biggest deals of the year. But you never made me feel special. In fact, you made me feel very ordinary."

I was speechless.

Mr. McGuire continued: "Here, look at it from my side. I thought you were a bit young when you took on my job but you were enthusiastic and you did well. But I do remember you being late for one of the viewings." (That felt unfair, I didn't have a car and the bus was late. Of course, that was of no interest to him).

"You negotiated a reasonable deal," he continued. "And then I never heard from you again!"

I stayed silent. He took three pieces of paper out of his top drawer. "Except for this," he said, placing the pages in front of me. It was our invoice for the fees for the sale. "The fee was fine Paul, but look at the letters you wrote." The first letter went with the invoice. I read aloud. It was our standard letter:

"Dear Mr. McGuire,
Please find enclosed, our fee in respect of the sale of xxx for your kind
attention in due course.
Yours faithfully."

"Read the second one," he said.

"Dear Mr. McGuire,
We acknowledge with thanks, receipt of your cheque, in full payment of our
invoice No. Xxx.
Yours faithfully."

"Paul."
I looked up.
"Who talks like that? You don't. Nobody does. Those letters sound like
they were written by a robot. They leave me cold! And, by the way, where
you address someone by name, you should finish 'Yours sincerely'."
Ouch.
"Paul, I was one of your company's biggest clients that year. I
remember going into your reception to deliver my cheque. I asked for you,
to see were you there, to thank you. No-one on reception had any idea
who I was. I certainly didn't feel special. I walked out of your office feeling
very cold. And then I got the letter from the robot.
"I never heard from you again. Until now. I didn't feel any connection
with your company. Just a cold professional relationship. Other agents
were ringing me offering me other properties but you weren't. You
must have realised that I would be reinvesting somewhere else. You had
the inside track but you never even asked me what my plans were."
I think he was feeling sorry for me at this stage.
"I'm sorry Paul, but you never made me feel any way special to your
company. You have got to make your clients feel special."
That was my hardest, and greatest, lesson in customer service.
"Make 'em feel special".
Meeting Mr. McGuire again just before my promotion was announced

had quite an impact on me. It brought all the right stuff back into clear view for me because I had taken his lesson to heart and changed my approach to clients. I went for a walk around St. Stephen's Green thinking about what I had just heard.

Then I made a decision. I went with my instincts. Nelson Mandela and JFK went into the rubbish bin in Dawson Street and I joined the function at the office. After the announcement was made I stepped up onto the plinth and I paid tribute to my predecessor. I followed on by telling everyone how I had just met Mr. McGuire and I told the story of his lesson to me in customer service.

As I was speaking I could feel that lovely vibe you get in a room when you know that you have everyone's full attention and that your words are having an impact. Mr. McGuire's advice was perfect because it gave advice to everyone in the company whether you were a secretary sending out a letter, or a receptionist, or a negotiator who needed to keep in contact with his clients. Importantly, it was a clear message to everyone there, from the porter to the senior directors, that customer service would be a core value for the company under my leadership. Afterwards, there was much clinking of glasses, good wishes and congratulations – but the words that really thrilled me came from two junior staff. "Now we really know what to do! Make 'em feel special!"

CANARY ALERT!

A good and fun way of thinking about your business's customer service (and of explaining it to colleagues), is Canary Alerts. A 'Canary Alert' happens in those crucial first seconds when a customer or client judges the service he is getting. Your customer/client is automatically evaluating the quality of the person they are dealing with. In other words – are you a Canary, a Robin or a Dodo?

Even if you are not dealing face to face with the customer at that time, if he experiences some work that you were responsible for, then he is also judging you:

"What type of person produces work like this – they're obviously a Canary (A Robin or a Dodo!)."

Sometimes it is a fairly clinical assessment: *"These guys aren't treating me right – I won't come back here."*

More often it's simply a feeling that the customer has at that crucial moment. Your customers and clients are always subconsciously evaluating the feelings they are getting at every moment as they deal with you. All those feelings and impressions are being stored in their brain. And all of those feelings will come back to the surface when they next consider whether to use you again or to try one of your competitors. Because each Canary Alert forms a link in a long chain of the customer's experiences.

So a great way to evaluate your business's customer services is to carry out a 'Canary Alert' at every point in the process where your customer/client comes into contact with you. Are we operating at Canary, Robin or Dodo standards at that crucial point?

Once we understand this concept, we are a long way towards a breakthrough. Every business has hundreds or thousands of 'Canary Alerts' every day. It happens every time your business comes into contact with a customer or the public. Take the example of estate agents:

1. Estate agents advertise property in newspapers. The public see these and consciously or sub-consciously form an instant impression about that estate agents. They will judge the design of the advertisements, the quality of the photograph, the text, the colours, the quality of print, the feeling of 'friendliness' and professionalism, the number of offices, the international connection, is the phone number big enough etc. So tens of thousands of these cutting-edge moments occur for each estate agent everyday, just from advertising.

2. Let's say our newspaper reader is interested in enquiring about a property and accepts the invitation to visit the agent's website. He now experiences another fresh crop. How quickly did the site load? How does it look and feel – bright and modern or out of date? How easy is it to find the property I'm interested in? How good are the photographs and descriptions? Does the site feel warm and friendly enough to encourage me to ring them?

3. Our enquirer calls the estate agents. How quickly was the telephone answered? Does the receptionist sound professional and friendly or like a bored robot? He's transferred to the negotiator in charge of the property. Again – for how long does the 'phone ring? How does the negotiator sound? Is he or she well briefed? Is there an offer to send me a brochure or arrange a viewing? Could I trust what I'm being told?

4. Our enquirer arranges a viewing. Driving to the property he passes other signboards erected by the estate agent. How do they look? Are they clean, clear and attractive to look at?

5. At the property was the negotiator on time? What kind of crucial first impression did he or she give? Smart, appropriately and professionally dressed and groomed? Friendly, enthusiastic and helpful. How were the introductions conducted? Smiling with eye contact, and the immediate offer of a card? All crucial Canary Alerts.

6. How knowledgeable was the negotiator about the property?

7. Let's say our enquirer calls to the estate agents for a meeting. What impression does the front of the office give? The signage? The window display? How did the receptionist greet him and deal with him? Was she expecting him? Did he/she use the visitor's name? What is the reception area like? What is the meeting room like? Is he offered tea/coffee/water? Many Canary Alerts.

8. Negotiations to buy the property commence. How does the enquirer feel throughout? Are the negotiations professional and trustworthy?

9. The enquirer buys the property and it's handed to solicitors. He receives a letter of 'Heads of Agreement' from the estate agent. Is the letter well-written without jargon? What are the envelope, the letterhead and the paper like – classy and professional or cheap and nasty?

10. The sale concludes. Does the purchaser or the vendor ever hear from the estate agent again? What would a Canary do?

So we can see how every business has hundreds of Canary Alerts every day as your customers, your clients, your competitors' customers and the public are constantly judging you. The more people you have, the more Canary Alerts are happening every day. Every single person in the chain of all those reactions plays a crucial role in how that customer will assess your business. The underlying key to transforming the quality of service you are providing to your customers is to make sure that every single person in your organisation understands that they alone are responsible for their link in the chain. Everyone must make certain that the customer leaves their part of the process having experienced a really good impression of your business, happy that they met some Robins and ideally delighted that they found a Canary or two.

It's also important that everyone realises that their unique link in the chain, no matter how small it appears in the grand scheme of things, can make or break that customer for good. Remember, Tom, Dick and Harry at my motor dealership. If any one of them had had the intuition or cop-on to see the problem developing and had made sure my CD player was fixed, they would have saved hundreds of thousands of pounds worth of car sales and servicing bills from me for their business.

It's also important to realise that just as a Dodo link in the chain in your business can cause damage and undo the good of several previous efforts, so too can a particularly good Canary moment reverse previous damage and save a customer. Imagine that Tom, Dick or Harry at my motor dealership had bothered to remember me a day or two later and wondered: *"Whatever happened to that chap whose CD changer wasn't fixed?"*

What if one of them had called me to say they would like to drop by my office and fix the CD changer and would that be more convenient than asking me to return to the garage? And after doing the work, they had then dropped the keys back to me at reception and handed me two recent pop CDs as an apology and as 'a bit of a change from Robbie Williams'. The whole thing could have been turned into a bit of fun with me fully appreciating the effort, the little bit of humour and personality shown. I have no doubt if they did that I would have formed a much deeper connection with that dealer, buying more cars from them and probably telling lots of people how great they are. Disasters, problems, complaints and bad incidents can be turned on their head into making people happy and loyal customers. All it takes is a little bit of initiative, cop-on and personality.

GETTING STARTED

The best way to get started with this in your business is to ask everyone to write down as many of these Canary Alert moments which arise in your business that they can think of. Have a good discussion about all of these – a few may be struck off or combined as other new ones are thought of.

Then try and break the group down into functions or departments which work together in dealing with a part of the customer's experience. Now have each individual write down as many Canary Alert moments they can think of where they are the individual who is influencing the customer's experience at that point.

At this stage each individual has their own list. Now ask them and/or their departments to think about how positively or negatively they believe each of these Canary Alert moments that they control will influence what the customers think of your company. Ask them too to rate their own Canary Alerts against how good they think their competitors are. Have them write a league table and maybe make a few calls together to some competitors and rate how your competitors handle enquiries.

We are now getting places. Now ask everyone to think about and write down how they could *improve* each of their own Canary Alerts. All of this can be a fun process but at this stage you can be sure you are making really serious progress.

Why is that? Because even if you retire to a cave in Alaska and this subject is never raised again, if the concept of the importance of these Canary Alerts has been properly communicated and thought through by your staff, you will already have a permanent improvement in your customer service, as most of your staff will never forget this lesson and this enlightenment.

Really raising the quality of your service requires you to consistently inspire everyone to come up with ideas on how they can improve their own Canary Alerts during their working day. How often can most of us Robins display our beautiful, colourful red-breast? Even better, how often can we get to Canary standards? Each of those ideas and improvements will in themselves be one degree kneebends; all small steps which put together will very quickly add up to something very powerful. Everyone working as one at making customers feel special, knowing what to do, with outstanding customer service being recognised and rewarded. Everyone giving 10 per cent extra effort – all leading to a leveraged, low cost and long lasting strategic boost in your customer service that will be enjoyed by your customers, marvelled at by your competitors, and will increase profits within a year. Beautiful.

EXAMPLES

The real joy of this process is that it is easy to understand and can be fun to go through. It also now has each individual member of staff thinking deeply about how they can improve their performance at moments which make the real difference to your company. This is a great level of awareness for a company to have. You now have everyone focusing intensely on the most important parts of the customer's experience. Just like a new TV, this really is 'high definition' customer service.

Each individual will have designed and set their own new level of performance. It's their own plan or customer charter and they will find the process stimulating and engaging. They will not want to see their ideas and ambitions for how they handle their own Canary Alerts as being weaker or less ambitious than their colleagues – meaning they will set challenging targets for themselves. That's important because now you have the glorious situation where your staff are almost competing to see how they can best improve themselves when it matters most to your firm. They're judging it by their own targets and that's far more robust and believable than if management suddenly announced a new set of targets to be reached without involving the staff.

Once you've achieved this jump in performance you should now look at how you can make it last – or even better improve it even more. How do you measure how you're doing? If you ask most companies they will say that they value customer service as a priority and that they provide very good customer service. If you press them and ask them how do they know this they'll eventually come up with: "Well, we don't get many complaints." That's as much as they know about the most crucial part of their business.

I think a good tuned-in manager who is honestly and openly prepared to look for weaknesses in his area, will 'know' when his team are really on top of their game. He'll hear it all around him in the phone conversations, meetings and contact with clients. In a manufacturing operation it's easier collate data on quality as there'll be statistics on defects, late deliveries, returned products etc. – although someone relying on all that and not talking enough to their customers might be making a big mistake.

For a service industry the best ways to measure the quality of your service, are by simply asking your customers and by 'mystery shopping'. Asking your customers to score you on their encounters with your company and your staff can either be done in a chat over a cup of tea or very efficiently via emailed questionnaires. This allows you to measure your performance as marked by your customers. You very quickly harvest a great resource of information and on a quarterly or yearly basis you repeat the process, compare your scores and you now know whether you are improving or disimproving.

Ideally, this can be combined with some 'mystery shopping', which is a process we engaged in at the estate agency – both because we felt we needed scoring on our Canary Alerts from the public (potential customers) and also because we wanted to compare ourselves with our competitors. A firm of professional 'mystery shoppers' was engaged and we agreed a menu of Canary Alerts on which we and our competitors would be marked. The 'mystery shoppers' made dozens of phone calls and visits to our offices and showhouses enquiring about properties or other services. Scoring was done in detail, on the numbers of rings before the phone was answered, speed of sending out information, quality of staff's dress, name badges, knowledge of the property, and whether staff looked for an opportunity to 'go the extra yard'.

They repeated the process with five of our major competitors. Imagine my disappointment when (while our clients were giving us strong marks), the scores from enquirers and viewers showed us as about average overall but far from being the best in some areas.

On foot of these findings, we got all the staff together and we revisited our Canary Alerts by challenging everyone to think even harder about what more they could do to improve them. We also agreed some other changes and then got back to business. Every quarter after that we saw a strong and rapid improvement in our scores. Where most of our competitors stayed at the same levels, we were ahead in most areas after six months and overall we could say that we were providing the highest quality of customer service in our industry. Always remember that you don't have to change the world overnight. If the industry standard of service is say 6/10, all you have to do is 'tweak' the dial to a 7 or 8, to be the outstanding company.

One area I took particular interest in was our main reception. In my view a company's reception and telephone answering is one of its most crucial areas. If it's bad (and lots are) it will do untold damage and lose lots of business which managers are not aware of. I found also that with companies increasingly having direct dial phones to voicemails/direct lines, senior management don't make calls through their own reception, consequently knowing less and less about what is going on. To take the example of the estate agent's reception, three full-time receptionists were needed to handle hundreds of calls every day into the company's head office together with a procession of callers to the building for meetings or enquiring about properties.

Fortunately we had a combination of three bright and enthusiastic girls who embraced the challenge we set for them. They came up with a great list of how we could make things better for our clients and customers. These ranged from very practical but long overlooked issues such as devising better staff rotas for lunchtime cover, to providing chilled water which they could offer to visitors, to company umbrellas they could offer to clients caught out in the rain. They came up with a map with directions to the building and nearby carparks which was faxed or emailed to callers. They pointed out that the reception desk was too high for wheelchair users and a lowered section was needed. The company enthusiastically engaged in as many changes as possible and our receptionists upped their game to fantastic levels, engaging brilliantly with every phone caller and visitor. One fantastic idea that stands out was that the receptionists felt it gave them such an advantage if they knew the names of visitors to the office for meetings. Obviously, we knew that in advance so it became the house rule that the names of visitors had to be provided daily in advance to reception with a brief description of the person if possible.

Previously if a visitor came in for a meeting, he would announce himself cold at reception and would politely be told to "take a seat while I call Mr Bloggs". Now, armed with the meeting time and brief description of the visitor (eg – "Simon Davis, London, tall, moustache"), the receptionist could leap to her feet as the visitor came in the door. "Oh, good morning Mr. Davis, you're very welcome. How are you? Did you have a pleasant flight? Joe is expecting you – let me take you through to the meeting room and I'll call him for you."

In the meeting room he is offered fruit, tea/coffee, water and a newspaper. The receptionist has now strung together a handful of high-scoring Canary Alerts that will have seriously impressed the visitor. He has been made to feel really important and well cared for, has the impression that the whole office was awaiting his arrival – and we now have a much better prospect of winning his business. And the cost? Virtually zero – it just takes attitude and a little thought.

"Make 'em feel special."

Our reception area managed to put the greatest gap between themselves and all our competitors on an ongoing basis as marked by our 'mystery shoppers.' From memory they got to an overall 8.8 out of 10 when the industry standard was about 4.5. I got huge pleasure from regularly hearing from a whole range of clients and visitors. "You guys have the very best reception I have ever seen. Anywhere!" Or the puzzled: "How do they always know our names?"

Remember the cost of all this – virtually zero once everyone has the right attitude. When you have your team members really enjoying coming up with new ideas to improve customer service, and getting a buzz from delivering them, then you are really on song as a business.

An important way to measure the quality of your service is to make sure that top management (and ideally the chief executive) personally meets with top clients at least once a year and with nothing on the agenda except service. The Pareto rule applies here and inevitably 80 per cent of your business's income will come from the same 20 per cent of your customers – so make sure you meet those ones, at least. This sounds easy but in practice can be difficult enough to achieve. You're busy, your clients are busy – there's a big temptation to casually enquire from the client as to: "How are we doing for you," during routine business.

The client replies: "Yes, everything seems okay," and the relieved manager ticks the box of having reviewed service quality with that client. That's not good enough though. If the client is busy or distracted he may not want to raise any issues. Sometimes even experienced senior business people can be reluctant to raise problems or complaints. It may be a 'feeling' they have or a few anecdotes they've heard that all is not right yet without evidence or examples they may not raise it. You are far better off knowing about it and having a chance to fix it than discovering the issues too late after you've lost that client.

The minimum that client deserves is a well flagged meeting with you (could be over coffee or lunch) with nothing on the agenda except the quality of your service to that client. The very fact that you are taking the trouble to do this will impress your client who will see that your heart is in the right place and your connection will be strengthened. The reason the chief executive needs to do this is to ensure that your business gets an objective and thorough feedback. Human nature being what it is, if these meetings are left to senior managers on a departmental basis, you are less likely to get back an objective and fully balanced report – especially if it is critical of a manager's abilities.

I was able to take the opportunity to show some major clients the results of the 'mystery shopping' tests on our staff where we were handling those clients' developments. I impressed on the clients that "if they were trusting us to represent them with their business then we would be constantly striving to increase our standards". The clients were "blown away" to discover that we were doing this work in the background and secretly marking details such as our staff's appearance, punctuality, friendliness and knowledge about their property etc.

It was sometimes even more interesting to go in with the "bad news" that our scores on one of their developments had dropped from say 7.6 to 7.2 but that we had identified the problem and sorted it out. Meanwhile, scanning down the report, the client could easily see that our competitors on his competition's developments were being scored much lower. One major client sent me a copy of a memo he had sent to all of his senior staff attaching our report on service quality. He was asking all of his colleagues to think carefully about what they could do similarly in their areas and threw in the line: "If we could take on board just some of the commitment to service that our agents are showing our company would be far stronger." Just think how easy it was to win the next competitive pitch for that client's next development. Attention to service quality pays off.

Better Customer Service Means More Money For You: I have no doubt that even in a recession many consumers will pay over the average price for something if they feel they are getting better customer service. Personally, I'll happily pay up to 10 per cent more for goods and services if I know I'm getting higher quality service. I spend about €2,500 a year on heating oil. I've tried various suppliers. Over 10 years ago my tank ran dry just before Christmas. Even worse, it was cold, snowing, and the roads were icy. The postman didn't drive up the hill to my house and my oil supplier didn't fancy it either. I rang Glen Fuels. They were friendly and efficient on the phone and said that their driver would try to get to me. He did and filled my tank – saving me from a chilly Christmas. I've used Glen Fuels ever since. This year I rang a few of their competitors and got quotes. One of them was about five per sent cheaper, saving me €125, but I placed my order again with Glen Fuels. All because their driver made it to my house in tough conditions some 10 years ago.

Surveys indicate that consumers will happily pay 5 – 10 per cent more than the going rate if they're getting better service. During my time writing this book I've had scores of conversations with people about their experiences and stories of great service. There's a strong theme to how people describe 'great service'. It's inevitably some small personal touch or effort which was unexpectedly added in by someone in the company providing the service. Or it's a particularly friendly individual or two that they just look forward to dealing with again. It's not a price reduction or a discount. It's the "little things", the "Small Steps", those Canary Alerts that usually cost you nothing to introduce into your service that will win you not only more business but more business at a higher price.

// CHAPTER 5 //
GIVE YOUR BUSINESS PERSONALITY

I'm constantly surprised at how ordinary a level of service is delivered by businesses which they think is good enough. Even in the depths of recession with businesses fighting for their very lives most owners/managers don't realise that as well as cutting costs, another option for survival is getting your customer service above the ordinary which usually costs nothing. It's clear to me that many businesses are not inspiring their staff about customer service. Customers and clients will return again and again to a business which they feel is doing a little bit extra for them, which has a bit of personality about it and which forms a connection. Remember – 'Make 'em Feel Special'.

It strikes me that the businesses I come across which provide that outstanding service and personality are usually owner-managed. The owner is usually a Canary, they're usually visibly on the premises themselves looking to get involved with customers and their behaviour trains and influences their staff who begin to step up to Canary status. Again, it's usually the "little things" that make a difference. What the owners are either consciously or subconsciously doing, is moving you from being a customer/client and closer to being a friend.

It's absolutely crucial to try to reinforce this understanding of customer service and my view that it's "the little things" that cost nothing that matter so much. This area presents such an opportunity for you. It is largely a question of attitude. The best way to do this is by giving you some examples from everyday situations which may resonate with you. If you are in business in any of these sectors you may find some ideas to consider.

I recognise that everyone else's business looks easy from the outside but many businesses have settled for a standard which they think is good enough but which they only get away with because most of their competitors are the same. I've thought through some sectors and to emphasise the importance of 'personality', here's some examples of good and bad service. I'm also now introducing the idea of a customer's/clients' expectations:

HOTELS

Remarkably for an industry that prides itself on service and hospitality, I can't remember one brilliant check-in at any hotel in the world and I've been in scores of them. The standard default check-in is brisk, formal, efficient and lacking in personality. They want an imprint of your credit card because they don't trust you. And hotels spend fortunes trying to get this right. There is usually no effort to establish some genuine friendly connection. Yes, most of them have copped on to using your name after they've seen it on the credit card but Robin receptionists don't look for an opportunity to ask you about your flight, the weather, or some topical event. Nothing. Sterile. And a fake smile. It's just a process, not a welcome.

The exception was the Park Hotel, Kenmare. Very friendly, conversational check-in. "I" was more important than the procedure of the check-in. I asked for directions to a restaurant in the town which had been recommended for dinner. From the receptionist's directions it sounded like it was a little further than a comfortable walk for me – but too short a journey to call a taxi. The owner who was hovering in the background obviously sensed this. "I'll drive you up," he said, coming over and introducing himself. And he did. Owner-managed. Canary behaviour.

Our expectations are usually quite high arriving into a hotel – we've looked at the fancy website, passed the flags and stars but invariably get the same sterile treatment everywhere. The hotel has missed a big opportunity to welcome you as if to their home and to make you feel special.

The standard and speed of service in hotel bars is surprisingly slow and 'sterile' and the more expensive the hotel the worse the service often is. As the late Hugh Leonard wrote: "There is one golden rule about hotels – the speed of service in a hotel bar is directly in reverse proportion to the fanciness of the barman's uniform." The Four Seasons and the Ritz Carlton are better than most.

About 10 years ago I stayed in a lovely 5-star hotel, The Grand Mazzaro Sea Palace, in Taormina, Sicily. One day I came back to the room and there was a bottle of champagne with a card wishing me a happy birthday. It certainly was my birthday but the card didn't tell me who had sent this present. I rang a few likely suspects at home but none had sent the champagne. Baffled, I asked at reception, did they know who had sent the champagne?

"Oh, but the champagne is from us. Happy Birthday."

Seriously taken aback I asked: "But how did you know it was my birthday?"

"Oh, when you showed your passport at check-in, we noticed that you would be celebrating your birthday during your stay with us."

Brilliant. Personalised and friendly. Make 'em feel special! I've never forgotten that and last year I went back to that hotel. It still has a nice friendly feel, almost like a family owned hotel, although it is part of a chain. There are cards from the manager with complimentary fruit and small bottles of port in your room etc., which is all great. But I've never met the manager. A lot of hotel managers spend too much time in their office. They should maximise their time out mingling with the guests. The manager is the captain of the ship and he should be out there recognising faces and forming connections with his guests.

The worst check-in I ever saw was at a large 5-star hotel in Dallas with maybe six busy receptionists. My own check-in was the usual sterile process but I stood and watched in horror as a bride in her wedding dress with her groom, stood in line for maybe 10 minutes, waiting their turn to check-in. Not one of the receptionists or various managers hiding behind the safety of their desks had the cop-on to jump out and take them to the top of the queue. No-one would have minded. No Canaries there.

At a wedding reception at the Dublin Sports Hotel when the bride and groom approached reception in full wedding regalia, asking for the key to their room, the receptionist asked; "And the name please?" (It was the only wedding party).

It seems to me that hotels make no effort to use the advance information they have to try to make your arrival really special. It must be easy enough to make sure the receptionists, porters, and managers on duty look at the list of visitors booked in to arrive that day. That will tell you how many people are in the party, their sex, family make-up, where they live, where they travelled from etc., etc.. You could check to see if they are return visitors.

Imagine a porter or a manager armed with the knowledge that the Murphys, a family of five from Kerry, are due to check-in that day. He spots a Kerry registered car pulling into the car-park at the likely time and sure enough it's a couple with three kids. Consider the impact if he rushes out to the car and greets them with: "Mr. And Mrs Murphy, lovely to see you again. You're very welcome back to our hotel. And how are all you guys this year? (Offering high fives to the kids). And how was the drive Mr. Murphy? Here , let me help you with those bags. And we have a nice cool drink ready for everyone in the lounge for you while I'm organising your bags and your check-in."

What a huge impact that would have. That would be like welcoming friends into your home. These guests now feel special, and will return again and again to "their hotel".

At a lower level even multinational chains for business travellers don't use the information they have. They'll ask you your name and then start tapping on a computer. They often don't even tell you that you are welcome and even though they know your address, they won't bother with any friendly, personalised conversation which could start with: "And how was your flight from X?" "And I hope you weren't delayed by the roadworks coming from the airport?"

Nothing.

Even in America, the homeland of customer service, while the training of frontline staff is usually good, you'll still get big variations in standards. Recently, while staying at an expensive 5-star hotel during a visit to Florida, we got a Dodo concierge. I couldn't believe it.

The body language and blank expression were a bad start. She had no enthusiasm for her job, showed no initiative and communicated poorly. Conversely, a few days later, we met one of the best concierges I've ever seen at the Sand Pearl Hotel, Clearwater, Florida. We were looking for a recommendation to a restaurant and information on shopping. He was a good looking chap in his late twenties, immaculately presented and his body language and smiling friendly greeting exuded confidence.

Us: "We're looking for a recommendation to a local restaurant, please."

Concierge: "Sure, myself, I love Island Way, it's just about a five minutes drive and you can sit inside, or outside overlooking the water."

Us: "What type of food do they serve?"

Concierge spins an i-pad around on the counter, taps the screen like a magician and photos of the restaurant and then the menu appear on screen.

Us: "Mmmmm, looks lovely."

Concierge: "Will I see if they have a table?"

Us: " Yes please."

While we're reading the menu the concierge calls the restaurant. It's 9pm on a Saturday night and we can hear from listening to his phone conversation that it's obviously full. But our concierge engages in some friendly banter with the manager and then tells us that there'll be a table ready for us in 10 minutes. He books us a cab.

Us: "And can you tell us about local shopping?"

Concierge, (smiling): "Of course, what type of items are you looking for?"

Us: "Mostly clothes."

Concierge: "Great!" He instantly produces brochures on three malls in the area and he can tell us which brands are available at which mall.

Us: "Mmm. Sounds like it's worth the drive to Tampa..."

Concierge: "Sure, it's very easy find it. Look..."

He magically touches his i-pad and up pops a Google map for the mall. He explains the Freeway route while he prints the map for us. He hands us the map with a big natural smile and spots the porter waving out of the corner of his eye.

"And your cab's ready at the door now. He'll have you at Island Way in perfect time. And is there anything else I can help you with?"

We gladly gave him a 10 dollar tip because we were delighted at the service and very impressed. This was a Canary concierge who loved his job, loved helping people, who knew that he was extremely good at his job and got a kick out of being as good as he could be. What a fantastic cornerstone for the hotel. Personality.

Travel Tip: *On your first visit to a concierge desk in a US hotel, tip the concierge at least $10, especially in New York. If you're staying a few nights, tip them $25 – you will have a powerful ally for your stay there and it can be a great investment.*

RETAIL

I've bought dozens of bouquets of flowers over the years from dozens of shops and can hardly remember any of them. Same flowers. Same price. Same experience. One day, a few years ago, I nipped into a new flower shop, Donna's in Donnybrook to buy flowers for my mother, who was in hospital. I explained this to a chirpy girl behind the counter who showed great concern for my mother and gave me a free gift of a ceramic angel to help her recovery. The next time I went back she asked me about my mother. I told her how impressed I was and she told me about herself.

Donna is a market stall flower trader from Moore Street. She gets up every morning at 5am to buy flowers. She decided she could run her own shop in a business district and she works until after 6pm every day. She told me she was called Donna after the song – so I sang a few bars of it. The banter developed and I now look forward to every visit. The last time I was there Donna told me I was like the guy in the film Benjamin Button, who kept getting younger. Reader – this is what ageing men like to hear. The queues grow longer at Donna's who is thriving through the recession, as other florists close. People go there not just for flowers but for a little fun and friendliness. Personality. Make 'Em Feel Special.

RESTAURANTS

For a frontline hospitality industry, the standard of customer service and personality is extraordinarily low. The arrival and welcome into the restaurant is so vital but most restaurants make little effort. Here's the normal default welcome: Two people walk in the door. Manager/waiter wanders over and raises their eyes, inquiringly. They might say "Hi" or "Table for two?" "Yes please," you say. "Sure," they say, turn their back, pick up two menus and walk away, assuming you'll follow them. You follow them to the table which they're indicating and sit down while they hand you the menus and disappear. Now at this stage you're usually keen to have a drink and relax whilst examining the menu but your waiter has disappeared back to their post. You wave to try to catch their eye a few times and then give up. Eventually they return. "Are you ready to order?"

"Yes," you say.

"Now, the specials we have tonight are…" pointing at a blackboard on a wall that you can't see.

Grrrrrr. Now you have to rethink your choice. *If I have the special main course, I might have soup to start?*

"What's the soup of the day?" you ask.

"I'll just go and see," says your waiter.

Why can't restaurants train their staff to greet patrons in a genuinely warm and friendly manner. Tell them they are very welcome. Did they get parked okay? Bring up the weather. Are they pressed for time or have they plenty of time to spend over the meal. Greet them as if they were coming into your home. Tell them your name. As they sit down, ask if you can get them a drink whilst they're looking at the menus – they'll love you for that! Before you go, tell them what the specials are – and the soup and fish of the day.

A Canary waiter/waitress will do all the above instinctively but why most restaurateurs can't see this going on amazes me. The recession has seen the return of a number of owners to the floor of their restaurant, as owners have to cut back on employing managers which improves things, but the general standard is fairly low.

The background music is usually too loud in most restaurants and waiting staff generally make too much noise banging plates. Remember, a restaurant is there for the patrons to relax in and chat – they're not tuned into the same level of noise and activity that the staff are. (The exception to above is Chinese waiting staff, who generally glide around without making noise).

Our Dodo waiter/waitress continues to make a few unnecessary interruptions – the first being to return with the food.

"Now – the soup?"

Grrrrr. There's only two of us, for goodness sake. Why can't 90 per cent of restaurant staff never remember who ordered what? It's worse where you have a group of six or eight, even in a business setting, where the waiter/waitress returns to the top of the table and stands over the group, hollering:

"The Pork?"

"Steak – medium?"

"The Fish?"

This repeatedly interrupts all conversations as dishes are passed around the table. Restaurateurs – how hard can it be to make a little note in your pad of who ordered what – maybe use a seat position, or "red tie" etc. Basic stuff but rarely done – even in the top restaurants.

Restaurants should always finish by offering a little something free – but rarely do. A top up of coffee? A digestif? Some of the Italian restaurants do, but it's rare.

GOOD RESTAURANTS I'VE FOUND

Chapter One, Dublin: Is a top restaurant with great food. It's not the best location, but it's main asset is the owner/front of house man, Martin Corbett. He always remembers you, greets you as a friend, and genuinely appreciates your visit. He has a great touch where he furtively whispers in your ear about some particular item on the menu, which is "absolutely superb" that day. "I had it myself earlier," he whispers. It's as if he's letting you personally in on a big secret, as a special favour. All brilliant. A natural Canary and the restaurant reflects his personality.

Emilia's, Enniskerry: Has a fantastic front of house man, Massimo. He's always there to greet you and he remembers names and children's names. Just the right amount of banter without becoming over familiar. Tops up your wine for free sometimes and always offers you a digestif (or two) on the house. They don't serve draught beer but if a group of tourists order pints, Massimo runs next door to the pub and brings them back on a tray. The food's fine but you go back because Massimo is your friend and the restaurant survives because of that, while others have opened and closed all around it. Massimo's a Canary.

Former Loves, Cork: A lovely upmarket restaurant with great service. First ever restaurant where I saw a waitress serve 15 businessmen around a long table without once asking who had ordered what. Later, reluctantly, she showed me the notes on her pad – she had tagged everyone by their ties. Brilliant. Simple. Free.

Camillos, Algarve, Portugal: Became a great favourite of my family's. Absolutely typical building, typical food, the same as dozens of restaurants nearby. But the piece de resistance was Don Camillo, the head chef, a big fat Italian man, who looked like Alfred Hitchcock and who emerged from the kitchens every now and then to chat with his guests in broken English. He wore a dramatic blue and white chequered suit, and an enormous chef's hat. Kids loved him. Everyone loved him and everyone wanted their photo taken with Don Camillo. The restaurant had colouring books and crayons for kids – resulting in peace for parents. He's retired back to Italy now, but a great example of how a restaurant thrived because the personality of the business set it apart. For free....

MOTOR DEALERS

This has to be one of the sectors with the best potential for a dealer or a brand to set themselves apart with their standard of service. Instead I find a poorish, very ordinary and similar standard throughout, with no real initiative shown to avail of all the interaction over the years with a customer. For some contrast, let's get back to the brand I know best, and this is an example of how customers have varying expectations of the service you're offering. You must know what your customers expect and better it.

My dealership opened a new servicing and parts depot nearer to my house and I tried it. The first problem or challenge this manufacturer's staff have is that they set such a high level of expectation of special service – with their branding, their customer charter, their brochures, showrooms, advertising, premium product and premium pricing. Therefore, when you get just ordinary service, you are disappointed. When you get bad service, you are amazed and angry. This new outlet did a couple of services for me and charged me royally – all okay, but they don't collect and return your car from your house, which another dealer I know, does. But the problems start when something comes up which is just slightly outside normal procedures.

My car had a few scrapes and grazes, mostly on the large plastic bumper sections, and a plastic cover over the headlamp washer had fallen off. My service manager walked around the car – "No, you can't touch that because it's plastic. It would look worse. You'd have to order a whole new bumper." He didn't know how much it would cost to re-alloy the scraped wheels. Jump forward a year, and I had a problem with the car and needed help. I left two messages at the garage, one on the answering machine and one with a person who said he'd pass on the message. They never called me back over three days and I got the problem sorted out at another garage. More recently, the two front headlamps washer panels fell off the car again, and I called back to the garage to order two more. It was wintertime with low temperatures.

Service Manager: "Were you using our special washer fluid with antifreeze in it?"

Me: "No, never heard of it."

Service Manager: "Well, they wrote to all the owners and they've been advertising about it. Turns out it's the very low temperatures that are forcing the washer covers off. So you need to use antifreeze washer fluid."

Me: "Well, they didn't write to me and they have my name and address." (They regularly send me lavish brochures offering new cars) "I think the main dealer should supply me with two plastic covers." (They're about €30 each, painted).

Service Manager: "Well, they won't do that, no way."

Me: "Well, they might when I write to them. What's the name of the managing director of the company?"

Service Manager: "Eh, don't know actually."

Me: "Don't worry, I'll look it up. Oh, and by the way, no one ever rang me back when I left two messages."

Service Manager: "Ah, I tried to ring you six or seven times."

Me: "I never got any messages."

Service Manager: "Yes, I just got interrupted every time I was dialling you. I never got as far as leaving a message. You see it was a bank holiday on Monday, so we had a lot of people in here with problems on Tuesday, so I was too busy."

Me: "But today's Thursday, and you still haven't rung me."

Service Manager: "Yeah, sorry about that."

Around this time when I heard the bad news about how nothing could be done about my scraped bumpers, someone mentioned that there was a very good repair shop called "Alan Mears" in Bray. Weeks later, I found myself in Bray, with time to spare. I looked up Alan Mears in the phone book. "O'Byrne Lane" was the address. This surprised me because knowing the town, I knew O'Byrne Lane was a back lane into a council housing estate. I had played football matches on a pitch down there. I couldn't imagine that a top quality operation would be on this back lane.

I drove into the lane, down the side of a pub, passed plenty of steel fences, barbed wire and the old sports hall I had changed in which was now burnt out. And then, next door, a bright clean sign – "Alan Mears – Motor Repairs". I drove into the small tarmacadamed yard, noticing a large shed on the left, packed with crashed cars being worked on and a portacabin office on the right. The first thing I noticed was how tidy the shed and yard were. Two men were standing looking at a car. I got out of my car, and one of them came straight over to me and introduced himself.

"Hi, I'm Alan Mears. How can I help you?"

I showed him the various scrapes and told him what my dealer had told me.

"Nah, absolute rubbish. The technology has moved on, we can make that like new – no problem."

We quickly agreed a price and the two days for the job. He wrote the agreed price on the back of an "Alan Mears" business card and gave it to me. I felt I was in good hands. When I delivered the car, they asked how I was getting home. I said I was getting a taxi. "No need for that, we'll drop you home" – and a junior did just that. I called to collect the car the next day but I was 20 minutes early. I could see three people working around my car in the shed.

Alan Mears Son: "Nearly ready, Paul, we're just valeting her for you. Come inside and have a drink – there's a match on."

Inside the portacabin, I found decent leather chairs, a satellite TV showing a world cup match, and I was given a glass of cold water. Ten minutes later the car was ready. The job was superb. I was delighted. And the car was valeted and the tyres painted and they'd fitted the missing headlamp washer cover which had been in the car. I got warm friendly handshakes and "thank yous", from Alan and his son, whom Alan made a point of introducing to me. I left O'Byrne Lane absolutely thrilled and super-impressed.

I've since sent my daughter and two friends there to have their cars re-sprayed. They're all delighted. There's no recession for Alan Mears. Several main dealers are queuing up to get their work into him and last I heard he's opening a second premises. The point is the dramatic difference in the level of service between a top of the range dealership where your expectations are high, and a backlane workshop where your initial expectations may be lower. So, the challenge and the opportunity is to find those little extra touches, that little bit of personality and friendliness which is above the expectation your customer has – and then you're on a winner. Alan Mears is a Canary and his son is a Canary-in-training.

PUBS

Again, surprisingly, another frontline hospitality sector which delivers very poor standards, certainly in Ireland and the UK. As spending power dries up and drink-driving and anti-smoking laws keep people at home, the business, as we have known it, is in dire trouble and pubs are closing down rapidly. In that environment one would expect publicans to be performing somersaults in a bid to improve the customers' experience in their pub, desperate to try to make friendly connections with their visitors, to make them want to come back again and again. But I don't see much of it. I see most pubs reducing prices, running promotions and adding bands in an effort to boost business, but they're not tapping into their biggest potential asset – their staff.

Sometimes I almost hold my head in despair as I observe the opportunities publicans and restaurateurs are missing as their staff deal with customers and the poor standards of service which the owners think are acceptable. Again the welcome is vital, a real opportunity as you are after all welcoming someone into your house, albeit a "public" one. In Ireland, the standard default greeting for a barman to anyone who approaches the bar is:

Barman:"Y'okay?"

Customer/Visitor: "A pint of Heineken and a pint of Guinness please."

Barman: "Take a seat and I'll drop it down to ya."

A few years ago publicans appeared to decide that delivering the drinks down to a table was a big step-up in service. It probably is and should certainly be offered but in my view it's now used by barmen as a quick way to shorten their involvement in the transaction. They pull the pints and leave them on the bar for a young lounge boy/girl to carry to the customer's table. This is a big lost opportunity to engage the customer in some chat, gain some "intelligence" about your customer – where they're from, staying, passing through, etc. Might they be back? Are they with a larger party? Anything they're interested in – they're often looking for somewhere to see a sports event or looking for some music or entertainment.

Usually any local will appreciate a little genuine friendly chat and the bar staff should be getting to know their customers. Tourists are definitely looking for chat and "craic" with locals and the barman should be a great start. Tourists love to tell you where they're from, where they're going, like to discuss the weather and the economy. Mostly, tourists get very little chat. Usually the young lounge boy/girl won't have the confidence or experience to introduce themselves and engage the visitors in chat (unless they're a fledgling Canary) and the pub loses a huge opportunity to add to their customers' experience and bond them in. This total lack of engagement generally applies equally to locals and tourists. And publicans wonder why their business is suffering alongside other entertainments.

Can you think of a pub where there is a genuine Canary owner, or manager, whose personality drives the business? There are very few. Sometimes you can get a stray Canary barman, who, despite the lack of training and poor standards around him, shines so brightly that his personality injects life and warmth into the pub.

The Harbour Bar, Bray: Recently won the Lonely Planet's 'Best Pub in the World'. It's my old local. It certainly didn't win the award for cleanliness but it has an eclectic atmosphere, rock bands in one part, fishermen, darts and Guinness in another. A group of 15 or so of my friends gathered there recently on the sad occasion of the funeral of a friend of ours, who had died in Australia. The Harbour Bar had been one of his old haunts. There were lots of old photos brought along, stories, tears and laughs. There's a new face behind the bar – a younger man. It turned out he was the son of one of the owners. He heard of the sad reason for our gathering and was very sympathetic. Towards the end of the night he arrived out from behind the bar carrying an enormous old canvas bound ledger. He said it had been there since the pub opened and that they recorded important events in it. He suggested that we assemble for a photograph and that we all sign and date the book, beside the photograph, to commemorate the death of our friend, David Carvill. He took great trouble over the photograph and it's in the book now. Guess where we are likely to go for our next get-together – whatever the occasion. Personality. Connection. Warmth. Friendliness. Connecting with your customers. Hugely effective. Zero cost.

Pubs Generally: Any business where there is a high level of potential interaction with customers is ripe for standing out from its competitors – because there is so much potential for small things to make a big difference. If most of the industry is at the same brain-dead standard, it makes it much easier to stand out. Here are some suggestions:

1. Recruit personalities for behind the bar and as floor staff. Demonstrate, teach and train them on engaging with customers to the right level. Encourage and reward it.

2. Toilets – big improvements generally over last decade everywhere but still too often a let-down. The expectations for toilets are now higher, given the importance of food in the offer.

3. When is the last time you saw colouring books and crayons in a pub for bored kids?

4. When is the last time you saw a barman take a tourist behind the bar to show them how to pull their own pint of Guinness? They'll gather in a smiling group around the beer pump and take photographs. It will magnify their experience and enjoyment tenfold. And they'll remember you, come back and send their friends. They'll Facebook the photo, with the name of your pub to hundreds of friends. Huge added value. Cost – zero.

5. Ever felt ripped off by the price of the soft drinks for the kids, or when you're driving? Smart pubs do cordials. Customers who feel ripped off come back as little as possible.

6. Why do about a third of barmen and lounge staff hand you your drink whilst holding the rim of your glass? Where you're expected to drink from. These are the same hands they're using for handling the money (and God knows what else). It's unhygienic and very off-putting to those customers who notice. I suspect most customers are too embarrassed to challenge the barman and refuse the drink because of the way he handled it. I saw this challenged once or twice and the barman looked amazed – I think they thought they were dealing with someone from Mars. This is basic, basic training and it's not being done in most pubs.

7. Pubs usually have some type of wheelie bin behind the bar where they store the empty bottles. So our customer wearily sinks onto his bar stool, relishes his first sip of an expensive drink, begins to read his newspaper, when suddenly CRASH – BANG – WALLOP – the barman flings a few bottles into the skip, a few feet away from the customer, causing him to jump a foot off his stool and risk a heart attack. This phenomenon is so common in the hundreds of pubs and hotel bars I have visited, (in the name of research), that I am convinced that the World Vintners Association has a secret training camp where retired expert cricket bowlers train bar staff in how to fling bottles at maximum velocity into the skip thus maximizing the noise and disruption to customers. If the bottle skip is nearly full and they can't get much more noise out of it, most bars and restaurants now have coffee machines where apparently part of making coffee requires loudly hammering metal parts together and the staff can use that for frightening the customers.

8. Publicans – why not put the cash register on the bar so that your bar staff don't have to/can't keep turning their backs on the customers. There's nothing worse than customers coming into a bar and spending the first few minutes looking at the backs of three staff in a huddle around the cash register.

9. Most people going to a pub want to talk to their friends. Publicans get in bands to try to boost business but the music is so loud that no one can talk... resulting in lots of people leaving. Crazy! I love music in a pub. In most pubs, it doesn't need to be amplified at all. Your customers will like the atmosphere, they can chat and the real music fans can sit beside the musicians. You can turn the music up towards the end of the evening when more people want to sing along.

The problem generally is that, like lots of businesses, the publican is too close to the business, can't see the wood for the trees and things have always been done that way. A lot of pubs could get fantastic feedback by doing some low-cost 'mystery shopping', just by asking some friends, who don't know the pub to come in and then report on their experience.

Great Bar/Restaurant Service: Recently I visited Tommy Bahanas, a famous restaurant/bar in Sarasota, Florida. It seats at least 200 people and it's packed most nights. I found a stool at the long bar and sat down. I was immediately impressed by the two barmen who were working flat-out serving drinks and taking food orders. The younger one waved at me as soon as I sat down, letting me know he'd be with me shortly. He said hello and congratulated me on my choice of the barbeque pork ribs, his favourite too. I asked for a glass of house red wine. He took me through five or six options and I chose Merlot. The meal was incredibly tasty. Fantastic.

The barman playfully looked furtively around him, leaned over and in low tones told me it was a secret recipe and that the secret was pre-cooking the ribs in Coca-Cola. He shook hands as I left. All this was going on as he worked at top speed, almost running from one customer to the next. A week later I went back. The barman must have served a thousand people in the interim. He recognised me instantly and greeted me warmly – "Ah – I guess you're back for more ribs?" I agreed. As he sat me down, he said, "Now, unfortunately, we've just run out of the Merlot you liked, but we have a better Merlot, which I'll give you at the same price." Amazing. He remembered me. What I ate. And what wine I drank, and used that knowledge to inject some really strong personalised customer service. And observing him, he was obviously operating at the same level with all the customers. Brilliant! I can't wait to go back.

A new pub opened recently in Greystones, Co. Wicklow, called "Mrs. Robinsons". It has a funky decor, low lighting and good music and no "horse racing from Wolverhampton" on screens. As we looked around wondering where to sit, a barman came out from behind the bar, welcomed us, suggested some seats and took our orders. The floor staff are pleasant and the toilets particularly clean. The barman called out "goodbye and thank you" as we left. We had a similar experience on the next visit. Some owner has seen the light and is training his staff well. Another newly renovated pub. "The Horse and Hound" in Delgany has also upped the ante with nice decor and above average friendly service.

Retail Generally: For the retail sector generally, it is so important to have the right, instantly friendly atmosphere in a shop. Yes, car parking, the shopfront and display are so important but if your shopper walks into your shop and feels an unhappy, uncomfortable or tense atmosphere, they are unlikely to stay long, or to buy much. Most of the atmosphere in the store is created by the body language, the expressions and the actions of the staff, in how they deal with their customers. I find that supermarkets are usually depressing places to visit – it's hard to find a smile and there's a tense, hurried atmosphere. I visit them as little as possible. I use both Tesco and Superquinn online and the supermarkets need to realise that their delivery men are the new face of the brand. They're generally cheerful and friendly types who do a good job.

A brand and operation I admire is Avoca where again you're visiting an often crowded store but I detect a policy of employing friendly, personable and attractive women on the various check-outs. They'll often admire what you've bought and always offer to gift wrap it for you, which is done with great care. They are a very important part of the Avoca success story – (which is not based on low prices), and the style and friendliness which their check-out operators add costs them no more than an average check-out operator.

I had an unusual experience recently in a supermarket in Sarasota. I have been working a fair bit in Florida and rented an apartment there. One evening I went to do my shopping at an enormous supermarket nearby called SweetBay. I approached a row of checkouts and a pretty girl in her early twenties who was working a register made strong eye contact and gave me a beaming smile.

"Hi there, how are you this evening?"

Me (noticing her name badge): "I'm fine thank you. How are you Katelyn?"

Katelyn (after a thoughtful pause): "Hmm, you know, I've been feeling a little strange all day. Just tired I guess."

Me: "Yeh, it sure was hot today."

Katelyn: "Oh my God. Are you Irish?"

Me: "Yes."

Katelyn: "Can you speak Irish? I mean, can you tell me what's on my foot?"

Me: "Eh, well, bróg means shoe..."

Katelyn: "No, no I mean my tattoo. I have a tattoo on my ankle. It's Irish. And I can't remember what it means."

Me: "Eh, sure, no problem, I'll do my best."

Katelyn (to woman in line behind me): "Do you mind if I show him my tattoo?"

Woman behind me (getting interested): "No problem, honey, go right ahead."

Katelyn (to cashier at next register): "Do you think it's okay here?"

Cashier: "Why not?"

Katelyn came out from behind the till, took off her sandal and put her leg up on a box to display a tattoo of words stretching down her calf, across her ankle bone and down her foot. An interested group of six or seven people crowded around, including the two grey-haired men who were filling bags, the adjoining cashier and two or three shoppers. I read out the words slowly:

"Beidh mé i ngrá leat i gconaí." It means, "I will always love you."

Katelyn (beaming): "Great, I knew it was something like that."

Elderly Woman shopper: "Jeez honey, you musta been really hammered when you got that."

Bag Filler: "Was that sore? Why'd you get that?"

Katelyn: "Well my great grandmother was Irish."

Shopper: "So was mine. Where was she from?"

Five minutes later, after a discussion about Irish roots and every word in that tattoo being re-translated separately, a beaming Katelyn was back checking out items and I left the store with a big smile on my face. Now the question is, was Katelyn doing the right thing or not?

In my view, she absolutely was, and any store manager should be encouraging all staff to maximise interaction with customers and use their personality. I have no doubt that the other shoppers enjoyed the whole thing and probably told lots of people about it. I'm sure it livened up the day for the bag packers too. And it formed a connection for me with a foodstore I know nothing about, and I did all my shopping there that week. Katelyn was letting her natural personality bring some fun and interest into what is usually a tedious chore. That's good for everyone – and good for business. So recruit personalities and encourage human interaction with your customers.

Unusually for call centre operators, I have found a high and consistent standard of service over the years from Sky TV. Conversely, I have had a wide range of experiences with Vodafone, ranging from diabolical, where they cut me off without any notice (because they had made a mistake with my account), to reasonably good. But I had one remarkable experience which is a great example of how one Canary personality in the chain, can save the day and make up for a few Dodos.

A couple of years ago, out of the blue, I began to receive monthly calls on my mobile, from Vodafone, enquiring how everything was going and usually mentioning that I was entitled to an upgrade or a new phone. I was impressed by this but it was only when I had a query regarding an overseas bill that I realised that the main purpose of the call was to sell me a new phone. Because month after month when I asked these individuals to post me a copy of that months statement they never did it. They promised they would but they never did. Around this time, I was considering buying an iPhone and I had costed them. Then I received a call from Vodafone:

"Mr. McNeive, we're offering a very special deal for iPhones this month. They're normally (something like) €449, but haggle with me, I can do it for €149."

Me: "That's not haggling, that's too easy."

Caller: "Well, go on then, offer me €249."

Me: "Okay, then, I'll go €249, and not a penny more."

At this stage, we both realised that we were re-enacting the famous haggling scene at the market in "The Life of Brian".

Caller: "€249! For this beautiful new iPhone. What an insult. I'll do it for €199. That's my very best offer."

We worked our way back to €149, at which I bought it, but it was the best laugh I'd had on the phone in ages, and it made up for the unhelpful callers over the previous months. Unfortunately, Vodafone didn't then put me on the price plan they'd recommended and then took several hundred euro from my account, each month, for the next two months. When I queried it, they saw their mistake and said it would take 30 days to recalculate my bill and refund my money. While I had been paying by direct debit for twenty years, to stop the system taking hundreds more from my account, Vodafone said they would temporarily put my account on "cash payments". Then they never switched it back to direct debit and a month or so later cut me off, without even calling me, for non-payment of my bill. Amazing. When after several calls and long periods of listening to machines I eventually got through to them, their customer care agent was intent on proving that the whole mess was my fault. So, very inconsistent service, but a good example of how one really strong injection of personality and fun can counterbalance lots of other bad experiences.

Seats Please: Most retailers still don't understand the importance of providing some seats in their shop. Shoppers are often accompanied by someone else – a husband being dragged along, or often small children. If the husband has somewhere to sit and read his paper, rather than mooching along unhappily beside the shopper, she'll spend far more time in the shop and will buy more. Similarly, retailers should make sure that there's something appealing to small children at their eye level in the shop window. Now, instead of dragging out of mother and trying to drag her to the sweetshop or rides, they'll happily go into the shop where a box of toys or a colouring book buys enough time for mother to buy what she wants.

Personality means more Business: No matter what business you are in, you must acutely realise that your competitors are selling similar or identical products to you. At very similar prices. So the only thing that makes much of a difference to your customers is their experience of doing business with you. And that is your opportunity. Can you be friendlier, more helpful, more fun? Employ personalities and let them loose....

// CHAPTER 6 //
CHAMELEONS

Sometime in the late 1980s I was working away in the estate agents struggling to sell commercial property through a decade-long recession. The more experience I gained, the more I realised that forming relationships with people – clients, purchasers and staff, and how you got on with everyone, was a key to success in business. It became clear to me that the best people had the ability to adapt their behaviour, as required, to best get on with whoever they were dealing with. This is a great social skill and Canaries do this instinctively. The estate agents was a great training ground for this because I found myself dealing with a huge variety of types of people and situations, often several times a day. This is where a good range of life experience, being well-read, and cop-on really stands to you.

This struck me one day when I found myself meeting the two owners of a scrappage business, in their yard on Sheriff Street in Dublin Docklands. At the time it was almost a no-go area, before the redevelopment of Docklands saw it at the heart of new office schemes. The site had become very valuable and it was important to connect with the owners in order to win the instructions to sell the site for them. People will not give you business if they don't like you or if they can't relate to you.

These were tough, down to earth, inner city, working class men, instinctively suspicious about estate agents in sharp suits but more than smart enough to know that they needed expert advice. We walked around the yard between the piles of scrap, ostensibly viewing the site but more so sounding each other out. My lucky break came when we went into the semi-derelict portacabin office for a chat. The walls were covered in three types of pictures – topless women, Manchester United players, and racing pigeons.

Me: "Ah, yeh, you see them on Saturday? Moran – world class. And McGrath's lookin' handy too." (Both Dublin-born players with Manchester United – safe territory).

This provokes a long discussion on Manchester United and various football issues.

Me, nodding at a pigeon photo: "D'ya race?"

Scrapman: "Yeah – big time."

Me: "Lovely check that. Is she yours?"

Scrapman: "Yeah, she's won from France."

Me: "Class." (Luckily, growing up in Bray, several misspent summers included catching failed racing pigeons on Bray Head, which we then kept in a loft and bred).

Intense conversation follows on checks, saddlebacks, eyesign, canker, corn v maize, and the Dun Laoghaire show. I left with the signed instructions in my pocket but in danger of being late for my next appointment. Ten minutes later I stepped into the Boardroom of KPMG on St. Stephen's Green for a meeting with two insolvency partners and two senior bankers about a possible instruction to sell a factory and site in Santry. It struck me that I was now in a very different setting. This meeting would have a very different atmosphere and tempo. I was going to have to adapt.

Me: "Good morning Gentlemen, beautiful morning – but the traffic was heavy."

Cue routine discussion on the morning's traffic as the teas and coffees are poured.

Me (addressing accountants): "The unemployment rate is really causing problems now – when do you think we'll see a reduction?"

Cue long discussion on the economy, a pet subject for accountants.

Me, addressing the bankers: "And I believe margins are getting even tighter?" (Bankers love moaning about lending margins) – Cue long exposition on the difficulties in the banking sector.

Presuming that you are well-read and up to speed on current affairs, you can chip in one or two comments but let them do most of the talking. The more they talk the better and the more interesting they will find you. The objective is to establish yourself as "one of them", and that you understand their business and their issues. Clients and customers must be able to relate to you, get on with you and trust you with their business.

Potential clients will sometimes "test you out" with some early statements or questions on politics or some topical controversy. They want to see what you're made of. So don't make controversial statements of your own – probably at all – or at least until you are very sure of your ground.

I am not a big fan of detailed techniques of mirroring people's body language at meetings, although it is soundly based. If your natural speaking voice is loud, and you speak very fast, you will have problems bonding in a meeting with two quietly spoken people who choose their words carefully and vice versa. Potential clients will be reluctant to entrust their business to someone whom they don't feel comfortable with, someone who "doesn't speak their language".

You must be able to adapt to the situation. This is not some type of pretence or trickery, it is a social skill. The bigger picture is to be aware that you must develop an ability to naturally and subtly adapt to suit the situation. Canaries do this instinctively. The first step for a Robin is to be aware of the skill, watch how Canaries do it, and learn.

// CHAPTER 7 //
SO, WHAT'S THE MOST IMPORTANT THING?

As I reached middle-management level, in the 1980s, I was becoming more aware of and more interested in bigger picture issues such as branding and the marketing of the firm. I continued to wear my heart on my sleeve in terms of the primacy of the quality of our service and building relationships. Then, we had an idea. A quality assurance scheme had been running in Ireland for a few years, called "The Quality Mark" – similar to a British kitemark standard.

Although quality assurance standards were born out of manufacturing industry, they were now being introduced into service industries. I was convinced of the value of being a firm associated with a premium brand of service and intrigued at the idea of becoming the first estate agents to achieve the Quality Mark for service quality. I will touch on the overall topic of Quality Assurance Standards/Systems later, but embarking on the Quality Mark scheme produced one very memorable lesson.

Now a large estate agency has a lot of different services and a lot of different clients – from accountants to bankers, to scrapmen, to private individuals to companies. About half of our approximately 120 staff were salespeople – buying and selling property for clients. The other half were in backroom services, providing valuations for banks, doing CPO work, managing shopping centres, administering rent and service charge accounts etc. In fact, quite a few of our staff were accountants. The point is that there was a very broad range of services and many different types of clients.

The basis of a quality assurance system is that you measure client's satisfaction with your service and work to continuously improve it. Our clever consultant explained that the first step was to work out what exactly our clients would be marking us on? In other words, what were the most important parts of our service, from our clients' viewpoint? What were our clients looking for? A meeting of all the staff was held and it was explained that each department should come up with a prioritised list of what they thought were the most important parts of the service they provided. This was, of course, a very healthy thing for everyone in the company to be thinking about. Also it was important that if we were going to start measuring our performance, then everyone must have an input so that they would feel part of it and be happy that everything was fair. This process turned into a bit of fun and there was plenty of heated debate about the prioritising of each factor. Everyone was asked to come back a week later with their conclusions. The next week, we all assembled in the boardroom and each department stuck a sheet of paper on the wall with their prioritised list and then explained them to the group. The suggested types of items which our clients would regard as priorities included:

1. Price achieved.
2. Speed of sale.
3. Professionalism and knowledge.
4. Accuracy and quality of reports.
5. Client contact.
6. Quality of brochure.

After some further debate and re-prioritising, every department now was certain that they had the right list for their service. We were making great progress. "But hang on," said the consultant, "That's what *we* think are the most important things to the clients. But we might be wrong. So before we launch our system, we need to ask our clients what *they* think." He was right of course, so we took the trouble to send hundreds of questionnaires to existing clients, previous clients and we engaged a company to do a street survey of the public.

The question was: "What are the most important things for you in assessing the quality of service from your estate agent?" We got hundreds of replies back. We were shocked at the answer. Yes down among numbers 2-6 there were our factors such as "price achieved, market knowledge, professionalism, brochures", but there was a clear leader at number one. And the shocking thing is that that one wasn't on any of our lists. And that word was:

"ENTHUSIASM"

When you think about it, doesn't it make a lot of sense? In any situation you will have great time for someone whom you feel is genuinely enthusiastic about whatever job they are doing for you, out there fighting as hard as possible for you and trying to get you the best possible result. Naturally, "enthusiasm" went to the top of our lists. It was a great lesson. Since then I've worked in a lot of different companies, markets, industries and countries. I don't believe that the paramount importance of "enthusiasm" has changed. Many a time I have seen senior successful businessmen charmed by the unbridled enthusiasm of an up and coming junior. I think they recognise some of the hunger that they had at that stage – they are drawn to it, and they like to see it working for them.

I have often seen mistakes made and forgiven as the client is more attracted to the overall power of the enthusiasm than they are concerned about a mistake. An enthusiastic Canary never makes the same mistake twice. Enthusiasm is infectious and has a great effect on other staff who feel the power of it. On the other hand a lack of enthusiasm for the job in hand and for life in general is the death knell for anyone in business. If a client finds himself saddled with someone whom he feels lacks enthusiasm he will look hard for the first mistake as an opportunity to rid himself of this blight on his life.

"Enthusiasm", from the original Greek, means a "person inspired or possessed by God" (enthusiast). That's how powerful enthusiasm is.

Enthusiasm. Remember the word and make sure you always display enthusiasm, ideally at all times, but crucially, always when pitching for work or when dealing with customers and clients. Enthusiasm.

// CHAPTER 8 //
PRESENTATIONS

The average standard of business presentations all over the world is very poor allowing you, with a little thought and practice, to become outstanding.

By "presentations" I mean any situation where your task is to communicate something to an audience. That includes anything from a meeting with a handful of people, up to addressing an audience of hundreds in a function room. I have witnessed scores of presentations over the years and only a handful stand out in that I have warm, strong memories of the presenter and his message.

Two of these were by Americans (perhaps no surprise), several by Watt Nicoll – Motivational Speaker, one by an Englishman and one by Sir Anthony O'Reilly. Others I fondly remember were presentations by some up and coming stars in our estate agents who were handpicked, trained and rehearsed into making excellent presentations to large audiences at company seminars. It was hugely rewarding to see how quickly nervous young people could be transformed into dynamic, professional presenters and to see the surprise and admiration on the faces of the audience.

Drawn from my involvement in presentations for many companies and from training and observations, at the end of this chapter I've given you a list of headings which you can use as your template every time you prepare for a presentation. But first, let's get a deeper understanding of how to communicate in this genre.

TELL STORIES

Ask yourself this ... Who was the greatest communicator of all in terms of greatest impact over the longest time?

Think big now.

The answer is Jesus.

And how did he achieve this?

By telling parables or stories.

What an amazing feat of communication – no e-mail, Facebook, Twitter or digital printing. Just pure and simple stories about people and events that the audience could relate to, easily remember, and could pass on to others. And each story carrying a strong message. Brilliant communication. The key point is that audiences will remember stories about people and events that interest them especially where you give them an emotional connection to the story.

The normal business presentation bombards the audience with small detail, charts, facts and statistics. Ten minutes after the presentation most people can't remember any of the information. But the presenter feels great because he got to show off how much he knows (or more likely, how much he can read off a screen in a monotonous voice).

Conversely, people can remember stories and can recall a surprising amount of detail from stories many years later. Just for fun, cast your mind back to a story I told earlier in this book. Do you remember the occasion where I was frantically trying to settle on what speech to deliver at my announcement as managing director of the estate agents? Do you remember what happened? I met a man, a former client. Can you remember what he looked like? What age group he was? What was he wearing? Where was the property I had sold for him? Do you remember any of the tenants? What type of property was it? Do you remember his name? Do you remember where we met? Most importantly, can you remember what this man's lesson to me was? Hopefully, you're now pleasantly surprised at how much of the story you can recall. On the other hand, imagine I had tried to explain customer service to you with a whole pile of statistics on the proportion of customers who tell their friends about good experiences verses the proportion who talk about bad experiences versus the proportion who will return and buy again verses the proportion who will or won't complain. You wouldn't remember it.

The key to brilliant communication is storytelling.

Politicians have realised this and are increasingly using storytelling to convey their message. Often at election time you hear politicians say: "I met a woman on the doorstep of her small house in Tallaght. She's a widow. Her eldest son was forced to emigrate to Sydney. Tomorrow, she will be driving her only other son, just 21 years old, to the airport also to emigrate to Australia. She is heartbroken. She is lonely. She fears she may never see her sons again. And that's a direct result of this government's incompetence in creating jobs. And now, this government proposes to reduce that poor woman's pension. And she can't afford her medication" etc, etc, Sound familiar? Storytelling to create a picture and make a point. But there's very little use of this technique in business presentations – and that's your opportunity. Find a story that conveys your message. The more vivid and memorable the story the better and you are allowed a little artistic licence to exaggerate the story. Can you give the characters and events 'hooks' that help the audience remember. For example, do you remember Mr. McGuire's enormous hat with a yellow feather, yellow tie and yellow silk handkerchief? The store full of artificial legs? All visual hooks, to help you remember the story.

STRUCTURE

The key to a good presentation is structure and here's the golden rule:

"Tell them what you're going to say.

Tell them.

Then tell them what you told them."

In short, after your introduction, you say: "Ladies and gentlemen, the three points I want to make to you today are: X, Y and Z." You then go through X, Y and Z individually and then conclude by saying something like: "In conclusion, I have shown that the three key messages are X, Y and Z and it is my firm recommendation that..." etc. So tell them what you're going to say, tell them, then tell them what you told them. Following this basic structure will help you write your presentation, will maximise its clarity and impact, and it will come across as well prepared and professional.

Before you start writing your presentation here are some points to consider:

1. ASK YOURSELF; WHO AM I TRYING TO IMPRESS WITH THIS PRESENTATION?

This is to force you to really focus your message on the right people. You should also remember that you'll probably need to impress your boss or colleagues too so an appropriate comment which acknowledges others can be generous and effective.

2. BRAINSTORM IDEAS

Sit down with a blank sheet of paper and write down every single idea or point that comes into your head and which might be relevant. Use a "mind map" drawing, like this:

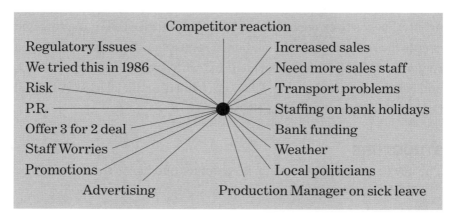

Involve others, as appropriate, in the brainstorming and in one sitting, you'll probably come up with over 90 per cent of the points which might be considered.

3. MAXIMUM THREE MAIN MESSAGES

Now choose a maximum of three key messages to convey. This keeps everything simple and easier to remember. You can support those key messages with some of the other points you thought of, but edit ruthlessly. Every point must make an impact and deserve its place in your presentation. It can be very effective to have just one, strong, clear message.

4. POWERPOINT OR NOT?

Ask yourself: "How am I going to make this presentation?" The standard, default business presentation across the world is done by using

PowerPoint. People are now sometimes very surprised if they hear that someone is going to make a presentation *without* PowerPoint. Now PowerPoint is great and unbeatable where it's absolutely necessary to show graphs, bar charts, pictures or videos to large audiences, but those occasions are rare. Instead, PowerPoint has become the crutch which simply helps the presenter to remember his presentation. Because all he does is read out sentences from the screen. I strongly challenge you to ask yourself – "Do I really need PowerPoint for this? Why am I using PowerPoint?" Some other problems with PowerPoint are:

(i) The audience is concentrating on the screen – not you.

(ii) Usually, the lights are dimmed – an automatic excuse for the audience to sit back and switch off. You lose eye contact with the audience.

(iii) You're stuck with your PowerPoint. More than once I have seen situations where, for example, in a competitive pitch for business something is said beforehand as the coffees are poured, which might make the emphasis of your presentation inappropriate. Or someone has turned up unexpectedly. Or some piece of business or political news has just broken and suddenly your PowerPoint is out of date. Typically, where there's a number of speakers, they discover on the day that they have covered the same points in their presentations. But it's too late to change and the audience is subjected to "as Mary said earlier", and "as John pointed out", which is amateurish and frustrates the listeners. PowerPoints are rigid and leave you little room to "think on your feet".

(iv) PowerPoints are prone to IT problems. On one occasion I saw a presenter announced to a packed hall in the Westin Hotel, Dublin. As he said hello he accidentally knocked a glass of water over his laptop which produced some amazing colours on the screen, a puff of smoke from the laptop and a cheer from the audience. End of Presentation. Many times I have squirmed watching business people arrive in a room to make an important presentation only to discover that their laptop doesn't connect to the projector or the screen's too small, or their lead to the power socket or the projector is too short. Or their laptop doesn't start up. Murphy's Law operates with a vengeance in the world of PowerPoint Presentations.

(v) The World No.1 Classic PowerPoint Presentation Mistake! If you have to use PowerPoint, don't make the same dreadful mistake which occurs in most presentations you will see. Typically the presenter puts far too much detail on each slide and then reads slowly through it, pausing on each point. But the audience can read much quicker than the presenter can speak, so you get this effect:

> • Key objectives include increased sales performance and increased efficiency by 8%
> • Staff organisation: By better deployment of resources, we can reduce staff costs by 14%
> • Focus on incentivisation of frontline sales staff with commission increased by 12%-15%
> • By the time the Presenter has read the above point, the audience has finished the points below.
> • Now the audience knows the content – before the presenter says it.
> • Now the Presenter is starting to look a bit slow and stupid.
> • Now the audience gets bored stupid, and more frustrated with each slide, and begins to resent the Presenter.

The solution to this, which requires a little more work and practice but which keeps the presentation lively and keeps you in control, is to use the bullet point function on PowerPoint. This means that only one bullet point at a time comes on the screen every time you click. That bullet point reminds you of what follows and you communicate that by telling your audience. This keeps the audience alert and focused on you. So the previous slide should look like this:

> Click ☛ Sales performance + efficiency
>
> Click ☛ Staff organisation
>
> Click ☛ Increase sales commissions
>
> Click ☛ **You're In Control**

(vi) A software application called 'Prezi' is sweeping through the world of presentations in colleges at the moment. It dramatically animates PowerPoint slides which now spin and jump around and zoom in and out. Most usefully, it allows you to embed videos in your presentation. The big risk, of course, is that the presenter becomes so enthralled with his fancy visuals that he puts them ahead of his content and his message will be diluted. Expect to see 'Prezi' before too long in the corporate world as an apparent solution to boring presentations.

5. WHO SHOULD PRESENT?

Normally presentations are made by the most senior person available or an expert in the area – but they may be hopeless presenters. If they won't respond to some basic training on how to improve, an organisation should strongly consider having the material presented by someone who is good at presenting as the impact will be much stronger.

6. HOW LONG

I suggest that 10 to 15 minutes is long enough for most presentations. Any longer and an audience becomes bored and overwhelmed with information. You should be able to edit your presentation down into those three key messages. In the world of professional speakers for conferences etc., there's often an expectation that you will speak for 40/45 minutes. I think it's too long. Even Bill Clinton, Desmond Tutu, Barack Obama and the best orators in the world are struggling to maintain intensity and impact over this period. It's far better to deliver a shorter presentation but which really hammers home your message. There's only so much your audience can take in.

I suggest a maximum of three speakers if an organisation is running a seminar either over breakfast or lunch which probably should be introduced at the start and closed out at the end by the MC. Trying to cram in any more becomes rushed, confuses the message and leads to a lot of messing about with opening and closing PowerPoint presentations.

7. CONTENT

Don't forget your structure. A presentation has three parts:
- **(a)** Introduction.
- **(b)** Three key messages.
- **(c)** Conclusion.

(a) Introduction

Keep this simple. Check what the MC is going to say when introducing you – they'll usually be setting out why you are qualified to speak on your subject and you don't want to repeat that. Audiences form an impression of you within seconds and as the old saying goes, you don't get a second chance to make a first impression. Hit the right note from the start. Whether or not you are using PowerPoint, you are the main visual before them. They will observe and evaluate everything you are doing even as you are setting up. You must "look the part". Make sure to check the dress code for the event and dress just above that.

If you are dealing with an American company, particularly in IT, you'll increasingly find the code "business campus". It turns out that this means T-shirt, shorts and sandals. Don't get caught out. Don't wear anything too flashy and watch out for jewellery which snags on microphones and equipment. How do you look as you are getting ready? Do you make eye contact and move closer to the audience to engage them as you begin. Even though you haven't said a word yet you have sent out several messages.

As you say how pleased you are to be here today to talk about your topic, it is important to come over relaxed, smiling and making positive eye-contact with as many people as possible. This starts the connection that you're seeking to make with them and keeps them attentive. A little bit of humour gets everyone to relax – maybe a reference to the location you're in or some newsworthy topic. Just make sure it is appropriate. Test it on colleagues or friends beforehand because ham-fisted attempts at humour can be a disaster and you don't need to take that risk.

Inspiration for good original introductions often comes from the history of the venue, a major news story, an anniversary or a designated day, e.g. World Woman's Day. As you begin, always mention how long you will be speaking for. This is an important courtesy to your audience who may not know if you are going to be on for 10 minutes or an hour. This point is usually overlooked. Make it clear whether you are allowing time for questions at the end of your presentation, or after all the speakers have finished, or indeed, if you're happy to deal with questions during your presentation.

(b) Three Key Messages

The main body of your presentation is your three key messages – and you can tell them just that. Can you tell stories that convey these messages memorably?

(c) Conclusion

Now it's time to "tell 'em what you told 'em!" You thank your audience for their attention, remind them of the three key points which you have made and leave them with a good closing line which automatically brings on a round of applause.

8. GOLDPLATE YOUR PRESENTATION

A really strong way to make your presentation stand out as well structured and professionally prepared and appropriate is to use a literary device called "topping and tailing". This is used almost every day by the leading newspaper columnists in writing their opinion pieces. Have a look at today's broadsheets and I bet you'll spot it. With this device, the writer opens by creating an image or making a memorable point which seems disconnected to the main story. Then, in concluding, they refer back to that unusual image.

This is a very powerful technique, which 'wraps the whole parcel up in a bow'. It helps the audience remember the story, makes the writing look very structured and signals the clear end of the piece. For example, I remember a very serious article about the troubles in the motor industry in America and high unemployment in some 'motor' cities. The article went something like this:

"I remember my first big car crash. My red Ford Mustang wobbled out of a power slide at 120 mph exiting my bedroom, and collided with my brother John's hand, which was reversing a Dodge Pickup. He was four years old and he screamed the house down. "Just wait 'til your father gets home', threatened my Mom." "Today, in America, unemployment in the Motor Cities"– continues the main article.

The conclusion: I still have that toy red Ford Mustang, but they don't make the real ones any more in our town. Dad came home from work but let me off with a scolding. Not long after, he stayed home all the time because the Ford Factory closed."

Do you see how powerfully this technique pulls the whole thing together? Successful use of this device alone will dramatically improve your presentations. Here is another example from another presentation which combines this technique with a strong sense of place, in the introduction.

The occasion was an annual business breakfast seminar for approximately 250 guests. The theme of the seminar was 'Our Changing World'. The venue turned out to be The Round Room, a large room attached to the Lord Mayor's house in Dublin which is available to hire for events. The Round Room was, in fact, the venue for the first meeting of the first Irish Parliament 'Dail Eireann', at which the Irish republic was declared and a provisional constitution announced. Home run!

So the introduction was along the lines of – "Ladies and gentlemen, you are warmly welcome to our seminar in this historic room where we will attempt to predict the future. One wonders if the 27 MPs who formed the Irish Republic in this very room on the 21st January 1919 could have had any idea of the changes that would affect Ireland over the following decades?

Then after the main body of the presentation the conclusion was something like -

"And so Ladies and gentlemen, as you have seen, we are predicting great changes affecting our lives over the next 20 years. But just as those 27 visionary politicians who launched a new Ireland from this room could hardly have predicted how Ireland would look today, we should accept that we can only underestimate the changes facing Ireland. They, and we, could only be sure of one thing. There will be change."

Again, you can see the 'topping and tailing' of the presentation, making it memorable and structured and conveying a sense of place. Practise this technique; it's a big step towards being outstanding.

Once you have prepared your presentation, then you practise, practise and practise. Practise in front of colleagues. Check your timing. Ask them which parts are most memorable. Are there any parts that confused them or seemed weak. Always try to arrange a dress rehearsal in the actual room or hall where you'll be speaking. Get the feel of the stage and get used to the sound of your own voice in the room. In the days before and especially the hours before you make your presentation, visualise yourself up there on the podium speaking. Visualise yourself looking and sounding great – professional, dynamic and well prepared. Visualise your audience being very very impressed.

Now, learn it off by heart. No more standing like a robot at a podium, reading out the slides. You don't have to remember it word for word and if you're using PowerPoint, the bullet points will remind you of what follows. Always carry the bullet point version of your presentation on a few cards in your hand. It's entirely acceptable to refer to them from time to time to keep you on track. If you have a complete brainfreeze or the IT breaks down those cards are your safety net.

Sir Anthony O'Reilly is seen as one of the great public speakers as well as being a gifted mimic and raconteur. It all appears effortless, almost "off the cuff". But I have seen the huge amount of preparation and practice that Sir Anthony puts into every speaking event, no matter how small. Every 'ad-lib' and story is heavily rehearsed so that his delivery becomes effortless and charismatic. That's called professionalism.

Once you know your presentation off by heart you no longer have to stand rooted to the spot where you can see slides on a laptop. You are free to move around the stage or walk around the room as you speak, maximising eye contact and the connection with your audience. If you're using a PA, use a clip-on radio mike but always practice with this first. Your audience will be riveted. You'll be the stand-out speaker of the day.

You're now seen as a great communicator, a great presenter. Indeed your entire stock rises. And all it took was to keep your presentation simple with lots of practice. You're outstanding.

I have summarised this Chapter for you in a Template, which you can use when preparing your next presentation.

PRESENTATION TEMPLATE

1. Who are you trying to impress?

2. Which presenters?

3. PowerPoint or not? Use bullet points.

4. Brainstorm Ideas. Use Mindmap.

5. Structure: "Tell them what you're going to say" (Introduction)
   "Tell them" (Main Body)
   "Then tell them what you told them." (Conclusion)

6. Pick three key messages : Can you tell stories?

7. Top and tail. Write a strong conclusion that summarises the main points. Link your conclusion to your introduction.

8. Use prompt cards. Learn if off. Practise. Practise. Practise.

9. Seek opportunity for dress rehearsal in actual venue.

10. Check out any IT issues days in advance. Have contingency plans for IT failures.

11. Visualise your successful delivery.

12. Be enthusiastic, positive and confident.

13. Maximise eye contact. Vary tone of voice. Move around. Pose questions to the audience to keep them engaged.

14. Invite questions.

// CHAPTER 9 //
WINNING MORE PITCHES AND TENDERS

More and more contracts are being awarded following a competitive pitching or tender process. For the state sector, this is largely driven by legislation. In the private sector, you need to be aware that the company offering the work sees this process as (a) a good way of getting the lowest fee/price and (b) is quite likely to take a selection of the best ideas offered by the unsuccessful tenderers and tell the successful bidder to use them too.

Firstly, let's distinguish between "pitches" and "tenders". To my mind, a tender is a formal quote probably to a state body but in a very prescriptive or box-ticking format. The body awarding the contract knows exactly what service they want provided and if you tick all the boxes, the job is usually awarded to the lowest fee or price. The terms of the tender procedure preclude any contacts outside the process and the format in which you must submit your tender is strictly laid out. Indeed, any attempt to vary the terms of the tender process may see you disqualified. In this instance, there is far less potential to set yourself apart from the competition and therefore I am going to concentrate on how to win more 'pitches'.

Pitches are where a private body (a company, an institution, individuals or syndicates) hold a competitive process for the awarding of a job or contract. For simplicity, let's call them 'The Principal'. However, while there is some instruction laid out as to the procedure for the pitch and the areas The Principal wants to see covered, there is plenty of room for manoeuvre and potential to stand out from the crowd.

A typical invitation to pitch for work includes a basic briefing, a latest date for receipt of your written submission and usually a date for a 'beauty parade', where you are required to present your submission to the group of people who will be awarding the contract. The Principal is less likely to award the job based on the lowest fee only. They are looking for creativity in your response and want to see how you will bring something extra – added value – to them. Particularly for longer contracts, at least some of the people on the interviewing board will be working with you, and it is crucial for them to feel that you will be easy and pleasant to work with. Even fun to work with.

As I did for 'presentations', I'm going to take you step by step through the process and at the end of the chapter, I've given you a template which you might adapt as appropriate for your organisation and which you can then type-up, circulate and use as a checklist for your next pitch. First, here are some things to remember:

(a) Great news

I have participated in scores of competitive pitches, both pitching and on the principal's side. Almost all pitches look, sound and feel the same, with very little creativity. With a little effort there is a great opportunity to be outstanding, and to win most of the pitches you go for.

(b) The job will be award by people. Humans...

Not by computers or machines. So maximizing the human connection throughout the pitching process is vital.

(c) We all look the same

The organisation awarding the job has assumed you have the skills to do the work. But no matter what product or service you are providing, (and particularly in the professional services area), to the market, you look just the same as your competitors. You have similar qualifications, services, experience, offices, publications and websites. Your people have similar names, backgrounds, suits and cars to your competitors. So the challenge and the opportunity is to stand out from the crowd.

(d) Panel beating

On a typical interview panel, a couple of people are highly engaged and interested in the process, a couple of others are somewhat engaged and one or two others have been pressganged onto the panel to make up numbers. Be aware that many of the latter two groups are bored to tears having waded through multiple long submissions which all look the same, and now have to sit through half a dozen boring and similar presentations. I'd go so far as to say that many beauty parade presentations are lost within the first three minutes. If the appearance, body language and energy of the group coming in to present is not dynamic and is followed by a waffly slide show about "our associate offices in Edinburgh and Kuala Lumpuar", the panel not only doesn't like you, they resent you and you're not going to win the job.

(e) Your success rate will reflect your effort

Like most things you get out what you put in. Of the companies I have worked with, every time we noticed a dip in the success rate of pitches, we discovered that we weren't properly adhering to our template. We had got complacent. A wholehearted return to the winning formula quickly gets you back winning more jobs.

THE TEMPLATE FOR SUCCESS

(a) Establish a Pitch/Tender Library. This is a basic first step. This is a bookshelf or cabinet where you will keep copies of all the pitches/tenders you submit and someone must be responsible for maintaining it. This will save you lots of time rushing around trying to find copies of previous pitches which someone partially remembers, but where are they? Importantly, you should estimate the total amount of sales or fees which you competitively pitch for every year. This includes both major formal pitches and less formal letters written competing for jobs. They are all pitches. You will probably be surprised at the amount of business you are pitching for. The person maintaining the library should keep a running record of your success rate so you know exactly how you are doing and you can track the success rate of different approaches and of different teams. (The library minder needs to have a bit of clout and savvy in making sure they get a copy of every pitch. Human nature being what it is, there will be a ready supply of "pitches we won", but less information on "pitches we lost.")

(b) Establish a Pitch/Tender Team. For smaller organisations, this might be two people, or for larger companies probably a maximum of six. These are not necessarily the people who will be directly doing the pitch. Their job is to consider all new invitations to pitch/tender and allocate responsibilities. This team probably includes a senior director and the Head of Marketing. The other members are probably those with the most creativity and enthusiasm for the pitching process – the more strategic brainpower the better at this stage. The members should usually be available to meet at short notice so we don't waste valuable time. If one or two aren't available that's okay. The imperative is to get pooled brainpower working as soon as possible.

A basic: Most tenders end up in a rush to meet deadlines for submissions. Over and over again companies waste time by allowing invitations to pitch sit unopened on the desk of someone who is on holidays or out sick or unread on someone's computer. You must have a system to ensure that these are picked up and the pitch team is alerted.

Another basic: Large volumes of invitations to tender for government work are published regularly on national government and European government websites. Many companies are missing these opportunities by not having someone responsible for reviewing these every day. Make sure you're on top of this.

(c) When an invitation to pitch/tender comes in copy the letter/brief to the above team and arrange your first meeting.

(d) Before the team meeting, members should have considered the issues below and should arrive with some ideas:

(e) At your first meeting, decide on the team for this specific pitch. Appoint the team leader who will be responsible for the pitch. This is not necessarily the most senior person in the relevant company department. Who is the most passionate, professional, driven person to run this pitch with the charisma and abilities to get the best out of everyone involved – and on time?

(f) When the actual team to handle the pitch has been appointed, at their first meeting, they should have a large one-page timetable. This is your plan and is the best way of keeping the pitch on track. Work backwards from the latest date for submission of the pitch, which we'll call "T". The plan might look like this:

Responsible	T-10 16th June	T-5 21st June	T-4 22nd June	T-3 23rd June	T-2 24th June	T-1 25th June	T= 26th June
John	Acknowledge Receipt. Seek Meeting	Arrange Site Visit	Brief Beauty Parade team	Draft of Presentation	Rehearse Presentation		
Mary		Brainstorm Ideas	Write first Draft				
Paul		Brainstorm Ideas	First draft of HR and IT input				
George	Advise Printers and Secretaries			Have all photos and CVs ready		Print submissions X8 copies	

This approach is particularly suitable for larger pitches with lots of people involved. It keeps everything on track reduces stress and avoids the usual curse of Murphy's Law where colour printers and photocopiers will mysteriously break an hour or two before the submission deadline.

(g) E-mail all your staff, advising them of the pitch and asking if anyone knows the potential client. Companies often miss out on the power of their own people and contacts. I once brought a junior secretary on a team pitching for a major instruction from a semi-state body. She had been well-briefed and prepared to deliver a piece on marketing at the pitch. The head of the semi-state organisation who was on the interviewing panel was her next door neighbour. We got the job.

(h) Before launching into writing your submission think outside the box. Is the client doing the right thing at all? Without confusing them, can you suggest good alternative approaches? Usually the client sticks with his original plan, however, you will score heavily for putting in that extra thought and effort. Any client will love to have his advisors bringing him 'added value' as well as just doing the basic job.

Think twice. Think big. Ask is the client missing a trick? Are we? A good example of a pitch I saw carelessly lost was where a supermarket chain decided to sell a redundant supermarket and land when they were considering a move. The instructions were pitched to three or four top estate agents. One of the firms was the dominant agent in that sector and in that location where they also had a high level of involvement in adjoining sites. The pitch was lost to a smaller agent who pointed out that a much better solution for the retailer was to do a swap of property involving the local garda station and some local authority land. Those swaps happened and the smaller agent won a delighted client and big fees. The large agent had all of the same information available in-house but didn't consult enough of its own people. Nobody saw the angle and the business was lost. Always step back and think. Can we add value?

(i) Acknowledge the invitation to pitch quickly and enthusiastically. Set a quick dynamic rhythm to your interaction with this client. The company which acknowledges last will probably be the slowest to get their tender/pitch submitted and will probably deliver all of their work at the last minute.

Try and differentiate: Imagine you sent the client an e-mailed video of your team at the location for the job or outside your premises thanking them for the opportunity, confirming you're already working on your submission and looking forward to meeting them soon. You could e-mail them a short professional video on the same day for a few hundred euro. Imagine the impact this will have. You're demonstrating your enthusiasm, your dynamism, your IT proficiency and you're standing out from the crowd. Another big advantage is that when they meet you they'll already know what you look like and they'll be more comfortable. A brief e-mailed video may not always be appropriate but when it is it has enormous impact when it appears on the computer of a client, particularly overseas. It's a real winner when pitching to anyone in the IT sectors.

(j) A Goldplated Suggestion: Find a reason to meet the potential client for clarification of something in the brief or for further information. Think of this; you would have a very good chance of winning this job if you knew the person awarding the job very well. You have a much lesser chance if you don't know them at all. The challenge is to get to meet them as often as possible during the pitch/tender process. A glorious opportunity to do this arises from the original letter accompanying the brief and the invitation to pitch. Invariably, the writer signs off by saying: "If you require

ABOVE:
My parents
Jim and Pauline
McNeive on
their wedding
day in 1961

RIGHT:
With my Mother
Pauline

SUNNY DAYS:
With my Mother on
Bray strand in 1964

COMMUNION DAY: At Elm Park, Dublin

IN THE SINK: At Ashbury Park, Bray

ABOUT A BOY: My favourite toy was that jetplane

GARDEN PARTY: At Dublin Zoo with my Mother. I remember this being taken so well

TOP GRAN: I was always fascinated with planes. With my late Granny, Ida Connolly

ABOVE: The John Paul 2, 1988, with John Glynn

LEFT: Playing guitar was prescribed for getting movement back in my hands

TOP: Paris 1988. We busked our way to Stuttgart to support Ireland in the European Championships

ABOVE: Butter wouldn't melt... Taken on the day I changed a dozen car number plates as a practical joke.

RIGHT: On duty at The Old Long Hill Bar

HOSPITAL DAYS: Recovering in Dr. Steevens Hospital in 1983. For months every bed I was in had a frame to keep the weight of the blankets off my grafts

BYRNE ULTIMATUM: On *The Late Late Show* with Gaybo in 1990. Note the first Jedward hairstyle. After the interview we performed "The Hoochy Coochy Man"

SING WHEN YOU'RE WINNING: At the recording of 'Watch Your House for Ireland' with the Republic of Ireland's '94 World Cup Squad

FLYING THE FLAG: Tired and emotional in Vilnius for Lithuania v Ireland, 1994

FLASH GORDON: Taking Mr. Darcy for a flight from Weston Airport

CHOP, CHOP: Final checks for a flight

FORE! Unfortunately, lifting the Ryder Cup didn't improve my handicap

ON THE BOARDWALK:
Speaking at the
Convention Centre,
Dublin

ANYONE FOR TENNIS?
My dad Jim at
Wimbledon in 2008. He
says he was narrowly
beaten in the semi-finals

HUGH TOOHY: Performing at Party near the Park, London, 2007

HAPPY 50TH: Performing at the 50th Anniversary of The National Rehabilitation Hospital

RIGHT: Meeting An Taoiseach. Edge was looking shaky that day

BEING BONO: With my hero. If only he knew...

HOLD ME NOW: One of Europe's best known singers and Johnny Logan

HAIL MARY: Meeting President Mary McAleese, with Henry Murdoch, Chairman of The Natior

habilitation Hospital, and Gay Byrne, keeping a close eye. I can't tell you what the President said

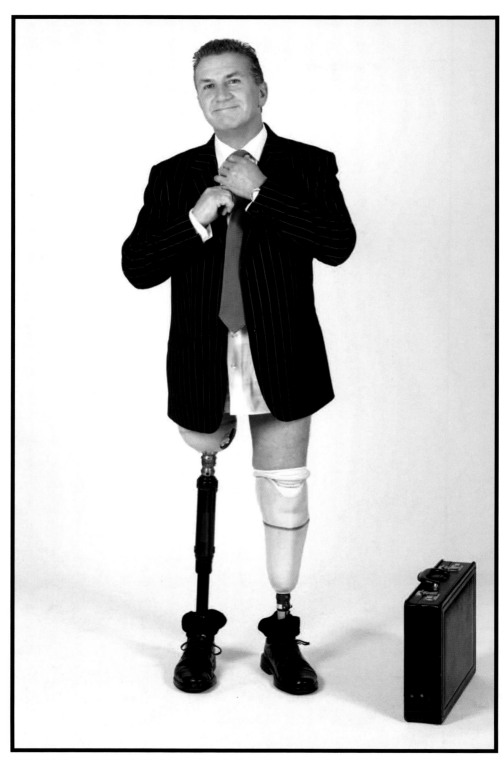

AS I AM: Legs polished. Tie knotted. Let's do business

clarification on any issues or further information, please do not hesitate to contact X". What an invitation. Yet, people pitching rarely take it up because they're too busy writing the submission. You have to make damn sure that there's something you need clarification or more information on. Call the writer and arrange to drop in for a brief chat over a cup of coffee. You've now set yourself apart from your competitors and you're getting to know the potential client. Clients are usually so interested in their own work that if you prod them with a few open questions they will launch into an enthusiastic re-briefing but this time they'll tell you lots of things that weren't in the formal brief. And they'll probably tell you what they think people should be saying in their submissions! Goldplated – don't miss it.

(k) Bring in outside expertise? Are there opportunities to strengthen your team's submission and add value by adding advice from another area? IT and HR are good examples. This can really help to set you apart, for a small share of the fees.

(l) The written document: You should make it as striking, memorable and professional as possible. Written submissions all tend to look and feel the same because they follow a traditional format. Make yours stand out.

✦ Don't make the classic mistake of wasting the first couple of pages by repeating their briefing to you and by telling them the history of your firm, the Edinburgh office and the Kuala Lumpur network – they know most of that and it's boring.

✦ Have an executive summary with every point both strong and compelling. No waffle.

✦ Maximise use of photographs especially of your people.

✦ Have standardised sheets, e.g. CVs of your personnel and in particular of projects you've done before. This saves lots of time.

✦ Don't bury your fee or price quote at the back of the submission. Don't be apologetic about it – put it in the executive summary. It's one of the most important pieces and it's annoying to the reader who can't find it.

✦ Make sure your submission is infused with enthusiasm for this job.

✦ Give real life examples of other successes and jobs you've done. Tell them your success stories.

✦ Maximise the use of testimonials and references both from other clients and from well-known people who are respected and influential to your potential client. These can be extremely powerful and they're easy to get. I've never been refused one by anybody. In fact people like being asked to give them. Where possible give direct contact information for your referees. The client is more likely to take them up and it looks more confident.

Stop and think about your approach before launching into your pitch. Read the brief. Find out who will be on the interview panel. Research them. Think about why they are there and what they might be looking for. A good example of this was a day I was on an interview panel to appoint a new firm of auditors to do work for a large company. A leading firm of accountants had been doing it for years but the relationship had gone stale. A new managing director had been appointed in the client company and he wrote to six firms of accountants asking them to pitch for the company's work through a written submission and then a presentation. The brief emphasised that a key factor in the decision would be to find which firm could generate the most new business leads and add value by introducing clients. The interview panel comprised the new managing director who wrote the above brief, the firm's financial controller (an accountant) and me. I had been pressganged onto the panel and wasn't looking forward to the day. Any basic research on me and the new boss would have shown that we were both salesmen or dealers with very little interest in accounts or tax.

Sure enough five of Dublin's top accountancy firms trooped in their top teams and all proceeded to bore us to death with identical presentations. They were all overlong, with someone from each area of their work droning on about financial details. It was hard to tell which firm was which by the end of it. The last firm in was BDO Simpson Xavier represented by David Simpson and one colleague. Simpson Xavier were the fastest growing firm in town. Their growth from two people in 1980 to 600 by 2005 was driven by the charisma, networking and ambition of the founders. They had a lovely balance of professionalism and the common touch. David Simpson introduced his colleagues, engaged in some friendly chat as the tea was poured and opened his pitch:

"Well you know that we know about audits and vat and stuff. What we'd really like to do is talk about new business development between our firms. I suggest that the managing directors meet fortnightly and as soon as possible we'll hold a function to get all our staff together and introduced."

Hallelujah.

They had read the brief and identified that two out of three on the panel were salesmen or dealmakers with no real interest in the details of audit and vat compliance. Simpson Xavier won that pitch by a clear mile and were in place many years later to earn large fees as company acquisitions took place.

Read the brief!

Almost every firm of accountants when pitching for work mysteriously introduces one of their tax specialists as being 'ex-revenue'. Nudge nudge, wink wink. The thinly-veiled implication is that no matter how dire your tax problems their man is a drinking buddy with the revenue people and can get any problem sorted out. There might be a grain of truth in it but it's quite funny to see firm after firm playing what they believe is a trump card.

(m) Throughout the process maximize opportunities for personal contact with the potential client or anyone likely to be on the panel awarding the job. They will appreciate creativity and enthusiasm. Could you take them on a site visit to a location where you could show them similar work you are doing so that they can "better understand your submission"? Could you offer to visit them to introduce your key staff who would be handling their work? Could you visit to show them a video? Or photographs?

A hard lesson I learned early in my career was in an ultra- competitive pitch to handle all the agency for Citywest which was a large, high-quality business park development on hundreds of acres outside Dublin.

Several major firms were invited to compete and make a submission for the business. The briefing document was long and challenging and very specific about areas that had to be covered in the submission. I was in charge and wrote what I thought was a thorough and excellent submission.

We didn't get the job.

The client kindly debriefed me afterwards. He said that what swung it was the other agent's video. They had made a video of other top class business parks around the world and had shown it to the client – before the submission date. He was so impressed with it that he arranged another meeting for the investors in the scheme to come in and be shown the video as well – again before the submission date.

"But," I protested, weakly, "The brief was very specific. It didn't say you could do a video."

"No, Paul, but it didn't say you couldn't," replied my not to be client.

I didn't make that mistake again.

Finally, if there is no formal arrangement to present your submission, then push hard for such an opportunity.

PRESENTING YOUR PITCH – 'THE BEAUTY PARADE'

For the presentation of your tender or pitch, often called 'the beauty parade,' all the principles of presentations in Chapter Seven apply. Your goal is to communicate your message in a memorable way, not to be quirky or inappropriate, but in a way that makes you stand out from the crowd and makes it easy for the client to choose you for his business.

(A) PowerPoint or not?

Ideally not in my view. For maximum impact, can we 'tell stories', which ideally touch the audience on an emotional level. Could we show a video? Use music? Use 'storyboards'? Appropriate video is extremely powerful. In the world of competitive pitching there is probably no bigger pitch than that when countries compete to host the Olympic games. It's a massive and long drawn out process of written submissions and site visits. London was ranked a distant third/fourth throughout the process to host the 2012 Olympics. Sebastian Coe and his pitch team then commissioned a video as to why London should be the hosts. They set aside all the technical stuff about finances, security, insurances, facilities and transport, and set out to make a video that went to the very heart of the Olympic Spirit – the inspiration of young people to take part in sport. At their last 'Beauty Parade' meeting with the Olympic Council they finished off by showing their video called "London 2012 – Inspiration". It's an emotionally powerful and moving piece of work. It's widely accepted as having swung the IOC vote to London. Have a look at it online, and then tell me that emotion has no place in hard business decisions.

For you it would have to be a big pitch but with digital technology you can make a powerful, professional video to support your pitch for less than €750. Ideally, show it to the clients yourself or you could e-mail it to the appropriate people or just send them a link.

(B) Storytelling

I really can't emphasise enough how important this is to stand out and to connect and be memorable.

A great example of a really tough but successful pitch I worked on was one among half a dozen estate agents to exclusively handle the leasing and management of a major new shopping centre in Ireland. The developers were Dutch and it was pre-funded by a German Pension Fund. We were pitching to a large group of Dutch and German professionals plus their London-based property advisors. This was a long-awaited pitch but initially we were not exactly confident. All of the competing agents were maximizing their various links into the potential clients but our main problem was that we had no office anywhere near the development and at the time we had no local staff to handle the scheme. We did however have an ace in that we had on our team an acknowledged star in shopping centre development who had great experience and proven a track record on other large schemes. Plus, we had a strong property management division.

We would really have to hook them with our success and experience elsewhere and demonstrate that we could replicate that locally. Although

I knew little about shopping centre leasing strategies, it was my job to lead the pitch. To educate myself on the topic I had a couple of meetings with our star man. He had been actively involved in the design and leasing of several large retail schemes and by thinking creatively had been particularly successful in bringing large international retailers into Ireland for the first time. As I tried to digest statistics on Zone A rents, footfalls and service charges I was soon struck by how entertaining and colourful my colleague's stories were about his experiences in landing these overseas retailers. For example, there was a hilarious and true story about a leading Italian fashion retailer whom my colleague convinced to visit a shopping centre under construction in Dublin. When they got on site in heavy rain there was a large pond blocking the entrance to the partly built shopping centre. Unfortunately this trendy Italian retailer was wearing white jeans and expensive Gucci boots and was reluctant to get wet. My colleague promptly picked him up and carried him through the flood. (They took the unit.) There were many more colourful and memorable stories which demonstrated our passion and commitment to our work while showing that we were at the cutting-edge of international retailing and had all the right contacts. Partly, I suspect, because we felt we needed to take a risk as we were an outside bet to win the pitch, we decided we would go in with a novel approach which became known as the "Terry Wogan format".

With no PowerPoint and no statistics on anything, the bullet points we wanted to make were to be written in marker on a flip-chart. Following a rehearsal that morning, we arrived at the venue to find a fairly cool reception from an audience of maybe 20 English, Dutch and German property professionals. The 'Terry Wogan' format involved me sitting in an armchair, playing the interviewer's role, and 'interviewing' my two colleagues who sat and stood informally either side of the flipchart as I took them through a series of colourful stories about their experiences.

Every time we had finished a topic one of my colleagues would rip the sheet off the flipchart, noisily roll it into a ball and throw it on the floor in front of us. (Very visual and very memorable, as the pile of paper got bigger and bigger).

Just minutes into the presentation, I got that beautiful tingle of knowing that our approach was working. The atmosphere in the room was electric with the whole audience hanging on every word, taking it in, being entertained and becoming immersed in stories about our success and experience. At the end there was a beautiful silence which was eventually broken by a German with a good sense of humour. Waving at the huge pile of balls of paper on the floor, he said: "Please, can we go back to slide number two" The room erupted in laughter and applause and we left on a high. Perfect. We won the job and many years later the firm is still running that shopping centre.

Worth remembering: While I prefer to win jobs by being creative and adding value there are times when it is appropriate to make sure that you win the job even if it means a loss making fee quote initially. You have to size up these opportunities, but I have seen many examples where just "getting your foot in the door" with a small piece of work can see you quickly reap huge benefits by being involved when a much bigger piece of work comes up.

In one case a firm I know won an advisory role to an organisation in the 1980s at tender for a fee of €9,000 per annum. That firm is still doing that work now for a similar fee but in the meantime has earned close to €2 million in fees for other work just from being there, being enthusiastic, professional and nurturing the underlying relationships with the clients. Because the relationship is so strong the client finds reasons to avoid re-tendering the work to other companies.

(C) Consider your Team for the pitch meeting

Bear in mind any personal contacts. Consider your numbers and don't bring too many. It may look like you're making a big effort but it's too hard to manage. Do not make the mistake of bringing people along, introducing them and then letting them sit there like dummies with no contribution to make.

Consider age and gender balance – try to match the interview panel to some extent.

(D) Consider the Venue

Ask the client for permission to inspect the room the day before. Check for IT compatibility. Ideally do a dress rehearsal of your pitch in the actual room. (The interviewers will get to hear about this and will be impressed). It shows professionalism, enthusiasm and commitment. Your competitors won't be doing it so you'll be standing out.

On the day, arrive early and double check any IT set up. Never assume everything works without trying it yourself.

Consider the seating arrangements. If you're in the room first or when sitting down after the introductions, maybe spread your team around both sides of the table so that you're mixed in with the interviewers. This dilutes the typical, sterile, interview line-up with two groups stiffly facing each other across the table. (All that's missing is a sheet of Perspex, like a prison visit, preventing contact!).

If you can get your team mixed up in a circle with the interviewers and all looking at and talking about some documents between you, then you are already a step ahead. The interviewers will feel that they are already working with you – not just interviewing you.

(E) Enthusiasm

Show passion in your conclusion. Finish by saying "and we would love to have this job".

(F) Rehearse, Rehearse, Rehearse

Before you present your pitch you must rehearse it – ideally to a group of colleagues. Colleagues can be briefed to play the role of the clients and should prepare some obvious difficult questions. You will be amazed at the difference two or three rehearsals will make to the quality of your pitch.

(G) Visualise the Pitch

You've done all the work, prepared your pitch and rehearsed it. Now you and your team should take five minutes together in silence and everyone should visualise themselves doing the pitch. Visualise how you will look and how you will sound: Extremely professional. Enthusiastic. Speaking very well, articulate, confident and convincing. Visualise your colleagues doing the same. Then agree how you are going to celebrate winning the pitch. Maybe it's a lunch in a good restaurant. Visualise what you will be eating. Taste it and smell it. Imagine the tingle of the first mouthful of champagne as you toast your success. Repeat this visualisation as often as you like. I always like to do it the night before a big pitch and again early on the day of the pitch. You will be surprised at how much this helps. As you are standing there speaking under pressure you will have this feeling of having done this before (a combination of rehearsal and visualisation). You will feel more confident and you will have even more belief in the strength of your pitch. You will sound more natural and convincing. Believe that you are going to win. And you will. Make sure to enjoy that celebration that you visualised – go and taste those bubbles!

SUMMARY

To win more pitches you are going to maximize the human connection throughout the process. Demonstrate enthusiasm at every opportunity. Now you have a better understanding of each stage; on the next page is a summary of this chapter as a Template for your next pitch.

PITCH TEMPLATE

1. Establish a pitch/tender Library. Track your success rate.

2. Establish an overall pitch/tender Team to allocate responsibilities and contribute ideas.

3. Appoint a pitch team for the job with one team leader.

4. E-mail all your colleagues looking for connections to the potential client.

5. Work backwards from pitch/tender date and allocate responsibilities and delivery dates. Use a one page plan.

6. Think outside the box. Is the client doing the right thing? Have we different ideas to add value?

7. Acknowledge quickly and enthusiastically. Set a dynamic rhythm.

8. Differentiate. Send an e-mail video acknowledgement?

9. Meet client for clarification or further information.

10. Add outside expertise to strengthen our bid? HR ? IT? Overseas experience?

11. Make the written tender stand out.

12. Tell stories. Optimise real life examples. Maximise testimonials and references.

13. Seek out opportunities for personal contact. Location visits? Show a video?

14. Push for a meeting to present your pitch/tender.

15. PowerPoint or not? Use storyboards? Use video?

16. Consider team. Maximise connections. Consider age and gender balance.

17. Rehearse, rehearse, rehearse. Role play with colleagues.

18. Consider venue. Room set-up? Seating arrangements? Have a dress rehearsal. Double- check any IT beforehand.

19. Team members visualise successful delivery of pitch. Now visualise the celebration.

20. Celebrate.

// CHAPTER 10 //
COMPLAINTS

We've all heard how important it is to be good at dealing with complaints yet I still find that many organisations are very poor at this.

First lesson: Times are tough and you need to hold on to your clients and customers. If one of your customers complains, BE GRATEFUL. The easiest option for your customer was to simply not give you any more business and for years to tell other people how lousy you are, thus costing you lots more business. You now have a golden opportunity to turn the situation around, hold on to their business and even turn them into an ambassador for your company.

The other night I was eating an impromptu dinner at a friend's house.

"This is lovely," I said. "Very tasty."

"Marks and Spencers," says my friend. "I always go there."

"Oh," I said. "Why 'always'?"

Once again, there was a story behind it.

"When I was a student living in Dublin 20 years ago I was always broke. Budgeting on a shoestring. Every week two of my meals were tinned chicken curries from Marks and Spencer. One night though I bit into something awful in my chicken curry. I spat it out. It was a big lump of chicken skin. Horrible."

"Yuck. So what did you do?"

"I wrapped the piece of skin in cellophane covered the tin and brought it back to Marks and Spencer in Grafton Street the following day."

"What happened?"

"When I told the assistant my story, she called for a manager. She was shocked. They were very sorry. She said it looked like chicken skin and was harmless but it shouldn't have been in the tin."

"And how did it end up?" I asked.

"She told me to take two new tins of chicken curry. I was delighted. Two free dinners. Then a few days later I got a letter from Marks and Spencer in the UK, apologising profusely. They had tested my sample which confirmed that it was chicken skin and was harmless. And they enclosed a voucher for £50!"

"Wow."

"Yeah. I couldn't believe it either. I was thrilled. That was a lot of money to a student in the '80s. Ever since then I buy all my groceries in Marks and Spencer."

You can see how clever Marks and Spencer have been about this. At every stage they handled this well, took it seriously and gave their customer back more than they expected. The cost to Marks and Spencer of the voucher to their own store was maybe £20. So for £20, they turned a complaining, unhappy customer into a lifelong loyal customer and ambassador who still tells this positive story about them.

This looks pretty simple and everyone senior in business will agree that this is the right thing to do. Yet that quality of response and initiative probably doesn't happen in their own company, or they only get about halfway there. Over and over again I see companies handling complaints badly. Apart from my own observations over the years, I've reviewed many 'real-life'"letters of complaint to national and international brands and there are several trends which stand out:

I. The larger the organisation is and the more layers of management it has, the more likely it is that handling complaints is just delegated to customer service staff as a routine process or administrative function. Even when a complaint is personally addressed to a managing director, the complainant often receives no acknowledgement from that person as the complaint is palmed off to a junior to deal with as an annoyance, or trivial matter, not worthy of their attention. This is at best discourteous and is also evidence of a management that is too self-important and has lost sight of the importance of customer feedback.

II. Do it quickly. The first thing a complainant usually hears is: "We're sorry for the delay in responding to your complaint/sorry for the delay in replying/sorry for the delay in getting back to you", but usually not giving any reason for the delay. Why? For goodness sake. It's as if the receipt of a complaint is a unique shock and they didn't know what to do. Be aware that someone who makes a complaint is unhappy and they will get even more unhappy every hour that goes by before you deal with their complaint. They may start out being annoyed but reasonable but if you leave them to fester they will become unreasonable, seething with rage and looking for revenge by the time you get back to them.

When you receive a complaint sort it out immediately. If possible and appropriate, telephone the complainant right away, take it on the chin and don't try to hide behind a waffly and insincere letter. The more senior the person that responds the better. If the chief executive can't be bothered to deal with complaints, at least have him personally sign a letter of apology to give the impression that he/she cares. Every chief executive should be reviewing lists of the types of complaints received.

Incidentally, Murphy's law applies fiercely in the world of complaints. If someone in your organisation through human error makes three mistakes a year, they will make two of them trying to sort out a problem coming from their first mistake. Chances are that if someone is asked to sort out a mess caused by a colleague, they will make their annual mistake on that case. This is usually because of the pressure and stress already surrounding the case and stress can make you stupid. Once a job goes off the rails it can sometimes be difficult to get it back on the rails. My strong advice is to deal with the issue comprehensively right from the start and this will save you time, money and customers.

Don't e-mail only. If you are making a complaint you are far less likely to get a good response, (or any response), to an e-mailed complaint. Even worse, large companies regularly do not respond at all to complaints made through Customer Feedback sections of their websites, which is appalling. I have no doubt that an e-mail has far less impact than a hard copy letter. People can ignore your complaint in their inbox and let it slip down the screen, but it's much more difficult to throw a letter into the bin or to leave it unanswered on your desk. Send a hard copy letter as well and always call up first so that you can address your letter to an individual. Then they can't ignore it.

If you're a business on the receiving end of complaints encourage a culture of responding to e-mails. Surprisingly many ignore them. Who in your organisation is responsible for checking daily on e-mails? When they are out of the office, who is responsible?

III. Particularly in the area of professional services, no matter what the complaint is about it will inevitably be swathed in complaints about non-return of telephone calls, slow return of calls and poor communication. The complainant will usually be right even if their memory has become a bit clouded by their anger. For heaven's sake once someone complains don't antagonise them with more slow communication. They'll be looking out for it.

IV. Don't just deal with some parts of the complaint and avoid others. That annoys your customer and they will never feel fully satisfied.

V. You must remember that just throwing vouchers or fee discounts at complainants may not on its own get the right outcome. A complainant might agree that they are "satisfied" but they may still not feel right about the whole episode. That's because complaints have usually become emotional by the time they are made. Hence the importance that all your staff react instantly to a complaint, that they show empathy with the person and take the problem seriously. Everyone must know that their actions in handling the complaint will probably decide whether the company loses that client/customer, or turns them into a lifelong loyal ambassador for you. The stakes are very high but most organisations don't act like they realise that.

VI. Make sure that your letter of response is perfectly written and presented. If you write a letter with misspellings and bad grammar you look sloppy and the complainant will get even more annoyed. With the availability of 'spellcheck', there is no mistake for misspellings, yet, many companies continually get this wrong.

VII. Many complaints arise from a lack of "follow through" on something that was promised. Also, sometimes a customer gets passed on to another department or office, but no-one checks up to see that the handover has gone smoothly. Don't assume that just because you have asked some department to sort it out that the customer has been saved. Follow through yourself, re-contacting the customer and make sure they are now happy, because, very often they are not.

With a little extra care and attention you can drastically reduce the number of complaints you receive and save yourself time and money. A key to this is to make sure that all staff realise that they alone are responsible for how that customer feels at their stage of dealing with them.

Another good news story comes from my work with ProAdjust, the loss adjusters. You may recall my telling you earlier that we also addressed the issue of complaints at our workshop. Just days after Martin Carway rang me with the great news on his 'mystery shopping' results, he called me again with the good news that another insurance company client of his which measures all complaints against brokers was pressuring him to help his competitors with whatever he had done to almost completely eradicate complaints. His clients survey showed that ProAdjust's number of complaints was now well below their competitors. The feedback from the insurance company's policy holders was that they "were impressed at the way ProAdjust respond to complaints and 'take control' or see the complaint process through."

FINAL VERDICT

EMPOWER: It's amazing how many companies don't empower and encourage their staff to deal proactively with unhappy customers and to use their initiative to make sure that the customer doesn't leave the premises or put down the phone feeling unhappy. Many organisations don't even empower their customer service staff to sort out unhappy customers on the spot – even for trivial issues. If the staff were empowered they could cut off complaints at source before they fester, holding on to good customers and saving loads of money and time. You may get taken advantage of every now and then by the odd chancer but they will be just drops in a sea of happy and loyal customers and clients. The objective here is to hold onto your customers and use the interaction generated by a complaint to turn them back into advocates for you and even ambassadors.

You will also reap direct financial rewards by training and encouraging your staff to "make 'em feel special", and to cut off complaints at source. People usually complain directly to the chief executive or at least send him a copy of a written complaint but I cannot remember receiving even one written complaint in four years of heading a company with 250 staff. This saved a lot of money in terms of time and potential financial losses and I put it down to staff, at all levels, seeking to make their clients feel special and resolving complaints at source.

Canaries know how to handle complaints intuitively and brilliantly. Train and empower all your staff to handle complaints like a Canary.

// CHAPTER 11 //
THE WEAPONS OF MASS INSTRUCTION - HOW TO WIN NEW CLIENTS

Over the years I have seen many well intentioned initiatives by companies to win new clients. This usually arises at the annual strategy meeting. Each department draws up a list of maybe six desirable target clients, then the flipcharts are taken down, the plans are stuffed into files and six weeks later most people couldn't name their list of new client targets. If there are a couple of new client wins during the year they're usually produced by Canaries doing what they do best.

The common weakness organisations have is a reluctance by individuals to push themselves to get in close with people in the target company. This means getting out of your comfort zone, spending time which is initially not earning money and being consistent about it. A question I often pose to a company is:

"Let's look at the list of the top 1000 companies to see how many of them are clients of ours?" (It's usually not too many). There are over 950 top companies operating all around us who aren't clients of ours. And many of them will have heard of our company. They will probably have a fairly good impression of us, from what they've read or heard about us. So, why aren't they using us? The answer of course is that they know someone in one of our competitors better than they know us. They may not know us at all. What we have to do is put ourselves in front of them person to person, enthusiastically and professionally, and begin to develop a relationship which ideally we turn into a friendship. Then you'll be getting lots of their business."

On a really simple level I sometimes ask: "Cast your minds back to your nightclubbing heydays. You're in a club with a few friends and you see a very attractive girl/guy at the other end of the bar. What are your chances of getting his/her phone number and going on a date if you stay where you are and just keep admiring them?"

"Zero" is the answer.

But, what if you approach them early in the night, sober, with a big smile and try one of your devastating friendly lines? Well, now you've got a chance! And even if nothing automatically clicks, well maybe now you know their name, and it's going to be even easier to chat them up next time you see them. And every time you do your chances improve!

Well, it's just the same with business clients – unless you make the effort, get talking to them, and get to know them personally, nothing's going to happen. But once you start trying in an organised and consistent way you'll be surprised at your success. For a start they'll see your enthusiasm.

When I was managing director of a professional services firm with 250 staff, coming up to the annual strategy weekend away, I would do plenty of thinking to set our priorities and targets for the following year. I knew that the best way to motivate people and to communicate our strategy was to keep everything memorable and simple – and to introduce a little emotion and fun. One year the winning of new clients was the top priority and I announced that we were going onto a war-footing. Each department, comprising say six to 10 senior and middle managers were given a brief to agree and pick just one target client – their absolute dream non-client who would produce the most fees.

They were to pick the best target client imaginable even if they had failed to win business from that client for years. They were also to prepare an outline plan, within an hour, of how they were going to land that client. To keep it light-hearted and on the "war-footing" theme, each department was given military or warrior uniforms with guns and swords. So we had a team of Vikings, American Marines, British Paratroopers, Navy, Gurkhas etc. Each team was photographed in their uniforms fiercely brandishing their weapons. We ended up with a list of maybe 10 target clients – absolute dream non-clients that we had failed to make a breakthrough with for years. Each team explained their plan and I was pleased to see a focus on new personal contacts to be made, opportunities to be brought to targets, invitations to entertainment etc. Each team was also told that they would be supported by the marketing department.

Back in the office one of our first steps was to set up a folder for each target client, which were accessible on the computer system. Everyone was informed of the initiative and invited to dump any information or intelligence on the target company into the folders, including any personal connections. When we saw the results of this we were surprised at how much we seemed to know but we had never pulled it all together. The marketing department were charged with building up a 'family tree' on each target and double-checking that everyone in the target company was on our mailing lists for reports, publications and entertainment. There were plenty of surprising omissions. This exercise highlighted a mistake many companies make. Frequently a senior person in your organisation is seen as your best link to a particular company. He/she may know someone there for years, may have got a small job years ago and may be entertaining them but is not getting much new business. That person will often jealously guard that connection, because they want to be seen as the link and everyone assumes that they are on top of their brief. When you get stuck in and examine it you'll find that your colleague's contact is not as influential as they used to be, the powerbase has shifted and the decisions are being made by others – who aren't even on your mailing list – let alone being personally targeted by you.

This led to our first basic step which was a complete overhaul of our intelligence and systems for each target. Each department plan was known as THE WEAPONS OF MASS INSTRUCTION and they were a series of small steps – "kneebends" towards landing those clients. Most of the steps were opening up new relationships with people in those companies but using better ways in. There was a heavy emphasis on face to face meetings. These target companies knew all about us and respected us. They just didn't know that we liked them so much and that we really wanted to work for them.

But the coup-de-grace was the giant-sized plywood board with a sign on top saying WMI (Weapons of Mass Instruction). I wanted to find a way to keep this initiative alive throughout the year and a real priority. I also knew that one of the keys was some competitive spirit. The board was a sheet of light plywood approximately 10 feet high and 15 feet long. It was huge, but could be folded and was light and could be moved around easily. It looked something like this:

WMI

TEAM	TARGET	
Picture of Dept in Army Uniform	Picture Joe Bloggs	--------------------Pic
Picture of Dept in Army Uniform	Picture John Doe	
Picture of Dept in Army Uniform	Company Logo	-------------------Logo
Picture of Dept in Army Uniform	Company Logo	---------Logo
Etc	Etc.	Cold warming
"	"	Blue --- Orange --- Bright red
"	"	Colour

The idea was that the picture of the target, either a picture of an individual, or a company logo, could be moved horizontally on a strip of Velcro. The left hand side of the board (the starting point), had a cold blue background, which "warmed-up" as you moved to the right, and by the right hand side, was bright red. The idea was that every month each team had to update on their progress and either move the target picture forwards or backwards depending on progress, to much light-hearted cheering and booing from the room. Meetings or personal contact with the target clients got you the best progress on the board. When you secured a job/instruction from the target, you could move his picture to bright red. The board was placed at the top of the boardroom at every management meeting whether on the agenda or not. You just couldn't escape from it. And one thing businesspeople hate is seeing themselves near the bottom of a league table. Especially with a picture of themselves.

Everyone really got their act together and kept at it. This was a list of 10 non-clients, the absolute dream clients, who had never given us work before. The first breakthrough came in March – three months in – when one of the targets instructed us in the sale of a shopping centre. The fees earned were approximately €250,000. By the end of the year, six of the 10 targets on the board had become clients. Never before has so much money been made out of a sheet of plywood, markers and velcro.

The Weapons of Mass Instruction Board, in various guises, has continued to produce the goods for me. A few days before writing this, a large professional firm I work with, had landed three new clients from a list of eight by May.

Select one target each – and go on a war footing.

// CHAPTER 12 //
LEADERSHIP

When I was asked to step up to the position of managing director the prospect was daunting, but exciting. At that stage I had been in the business for almost 25 years and while everything was going well I was becoming a little bored with the usual work. I was now routinely buying and selling properties for €30m, €40m, €50m and more; yet I needed a new challenge. Whether in good times or bad the leaders role is a difficult and sometimes lonely one. Very quickly I realised that while I had the experience and instincts to know what to do with matters relating to property or running the business, the hardest issues to handle would be human ones. For example, there were constant issues with retaining staff, attracting staff, removing staff, staff conflicts, staff deaths and illnesses and every possible issue that human interaction produces. It was tough going at times.

The big challenge for me was the separation of "strategic work" from "operational work" – and knowing the difference. As the leader, together with your board, your highest value work is in devising the strategic direction of the firm. But you can become entangled in all of the human conflict involved in taking two people from one department and moving them to another. This work however is operational, not strategic. Deciding to open an office in China and moving two people there is strategic. I think a lot of well-intentioned leaders become immersed in operational activity at a cost to their strategic input.

As I said in the Foreword, although I'm highlighting what I believe are the most important areas for leaders and offering some practical tips, I am not for one moment suggesting that I have all these qualities in abundance. In fact I know that I don't, but awareness is at least a starting point.

Thousands of books have been written on leadership – and millions of hours of training courses held on the subject. I've read a lot of those books and been on a few courses too. I don't remember a lot of that (which says something in itself) but outstanding among them was a very intensive week I spent at the London Business School, on a course called "The Essentials of Leadership". Much of what I have learned is from observation of leaders in the wide variety of organisations I have worked with and of course from my own direct experience. I'm going to summarise all of that and it may be worth dwelling on these points and considering their relevance to you:

(a) LEADERSHIP: The best definition I ever heard: "Leadership is inspiring others to higher performance." Have a good think about that. How can you inspire those around you, to "up their game"? Not "order" them to up their game. Inspire them.

(b) THE RIGHT PATH: The word 'leader' derives from the Latin word for "pathway". Leadership means finding the correct path to take and inspiring others to trust you enough to follow you.

(c) SELF-AWARENESS: This is very important and comes to many with experience. However, many leaders are too thick-skinned to realise the importance of their own strengths and weaknesses and the powerful effect of their behaviour on others.

Like most things in life there's a balance to be struck. Leaders certainly must convey confidence but an overly authoritarian self-belief will lose you followers. Authority is a poor substitute for leadership.

I would never have believed that I had certain characteristics until a healthy series of self-analysis and personality profiling began identifying some recurring themes which could not be ignored. Some of these took place at the London Business School and some were peer review, employee review and 360 degree profiling carried out at work. I was happily scoring well in all areas but there was a recurring feedback saying that perhaps I just seemed too damn good at everything.

That's just not fully believable – and it certainly doesn't help your employees/followers to identify with you. It can be a bit overpowering. For example I had a great record as a salesman and I was rising quickly through the management ranks. I was successful. I was flying helicopters, fronting a band, working hard and overcoming my disability. But I was afraid to show any vulnerability or weakness – and that's just not human. I didn't have to analyse matters a whole lot further to conclude that maybe

I was coming across as a bit over-confident. There's a fine line between confident and cocky. And that's not good.

It meant I needed to change. Without lowering any of my ambitions or positivity, I decided to moderate my behaviour and attitude a little and hopefully became a bit more "human" and "believable". This wasn't a contrived process because the belated realisation that I had this flaw was chastening in itself and I took it to heart.

This lesson resonated strongly with an early message at the London Business School which was that: "Leaders should declare a weakness – but make sure it's not one that's key to your core responsibilities."

The point of this was to dilute this somewhat unrealistic image of apparent invincibility that many leaders portray. Another interesting angle is that consistently "declaring a weakness" sees you identified with that weakness only – and deflects attention from any other weaknesses, which might be more serious. A good example was John F. Kennedy who repeatedly declared a weakness in mathematics. "I'm no good at numbers," he'd say, "but I have lots of people around me who can do all that. I'm more interested in the people." The result was that he was always associated with a non-core weakness in processing numbers whereas his real and serious weakness was for affairs with attractive women – and that wasn't highlighted until much later.

For my part, at my inauguration speech as managing director, I referred to "how lousy I was with IT. I could manage basic stuff, but fortunately I had a great PA and an IT department to help me when I needed it." This label certainly stuck and whether it distracted from other weaknesses or not I don't know. However, I've no doubt that it is a powerful thing for a leader to declare a weakness – it makes you much more human and believable to your followers.

Another very useful lesson from the London Business School was how powerfully a message could be communicated by using the "how I stumbled but recovered" technique. Here, in order to memorably communicate an idea to his followers, a leader talks about how he learned his lesson the hard way, how he had made a mess of something but then saw the light and recovered. This is usually a surprising admission of fallibility by the leader and is a human touch, acknowledging that we all make mistakes. The important thing is that we learn from our mistakes and do better the next time. Do you remember my inaugural speech where I told the story of how I learned the importance of customer service? How I made so many mistakes in dealing with Mr. McGuire? How I never "made him feel special"? That story is a good example of "how I stumbled and recovered", in communicating a message.

Another thing I started to do was to completely change my attitude to the first day back at work each year after the Christmas break. This was always a tough day as everyone had got used to spending time with family, relaxing, partying and sleeping on. During the dreaded first day back everyone was tired, worried that they'd spent too much money over Christmas and the office was invariably quiet and dark. Nobody felt like attacking their work. My instinct and behaviour over years was that 'the boss' had to be seen to be in early working flat-out, issuing instructions in all directions and generally trying to coerce everyone into doing some work. Maybe some people did a little work when they thought 'the boss' was around. I realised that people were going to do a certain level of work come what may and that 'the boss' charging around causing people to try and look busy wasn't achieving a whole lot.

I decided that I would routinely spend that day chatting individually with my colleagues, just wandering around the various departments. It was a perfect time to do this; to hear about people's families, their children, how they celebrated Christmas and the New Year etc. At the outset of the conversation I'd honestly declare how tough it was to get out of bed that morning and how it was hard to get fired up for work that day. That's exactly how they felt too and I wasn't going to make much difference by putting on my Superman outfit and flying around trying to look passionate and busy. Years later I got some nice feedback on these chats and it helped build a stronger and more natural connection with colleagues. By the second day back you're feeling more fired-up but now when you're asking people to start pushing harder and setting that example people respond more enthusiastically – we're all in this together!

LEADERSHIP AND VISION

A leader must have a vision of the future and you must be able to help others see that vision too. You must then be able to map out a plan as to how you are all going to realise that vision. Sound familiar? In essence the leader is the person who creates and pulls together my plan of small steps. The leader then inspires and motivate others to keep taking those small steps until you all reach your Goal.

I like this quotation from Stephen Covey:

"Management is efficiency in climbing the ladder of success; leadership determines whether the ladder is leaning against the right wall."

As a leader you need a clear vision of where you want to take everyone. You must communicate that effectively and inspire everyone to keep going until that goal is achieved. If your staff (followers) do not have a clear understanding of what you are all trying to achieve you will never get near their best performance. Your staff must feel that their work is a valuable part of the plan, that it is appreciated, that they are making progress and that their work counts.

INTEGRITY

As a leader you must always display the highest standards of honesty and integrity. Never swap a short-term gain or solving of a problem for any compromising of your integrity. This applies to your dealings with clients, colleagues, staff – everyone. And yourself. If you ever drop your standards of integrity you will eventually be found out and you are then flawed goods.

A DEGREE OF SEPARATION

A leader must have a degree of separation from his peers and staff. This can be a very difficult area especially for newly promoted leaders. For years you may have been close friends and drinking buddies with many of your colleagues. You can still be friends but you have to pull back a little to maintain objectivity and implicit authority. For example, how can you adjudicate on a dispute between two colleagues if you've been out drinking with one of them over the last couple of evenings? You are now compromised. So you need to take a small step backwards and establish an equal gap from everyone.

BE AN ENIGMA

Top leaders are often a little enigmatic; you can't always fully read them or always be certain what they will do. It's a good idea to maintain a level of enigma – don't always play all your cards up front. Don't always tell everyone everything about yourself. Keep a little space.

A COMMUNICATOR

Top leaders are great communicators. Everyone in your organisation should know what the organisation's values are and what the organisation's goals are (including their own goals). This sounds absolutely basic but this is far easier said than done. It's easier in some sectors than others. e.g. Ryanair = Low Fares. In Silicon Valley, some IT companies put their objective for that year or mission statement, literally over the door. e.g. "The world's fastest chip by 2015" or "Innovation". But for professional firms this is more difficult – and the larger you get, the more difficult it is to communicate any message. Malcolm Gladwell concluded in his brilliant book "The Tipping Point", that you need to get to a minimum of 150 people talking about your product, service or message, for "word of mouth" to begin to spread exponentially. The "converse" is true too because it's relatively easy to communicate a consistent message in an organisation of up to 150 people. But once you get over 150, it's much harder to keep everyone "on message". I think this is rock solid and it's certainly my experience and that of other companies I know. When a company starts encountering problems, more complaints or things going badly wrong, you'll often hear a shocked senior director say: "But how could they do that? How did they not know that that's not how we do things here"? The senior directors and the longest serving staff assume that everyone continues to know how things are done. When that starts going wrong you'll inevitably find that the numbers in the organisation have recently gone over the 150 mark. The message just isn't as "sticky" any more.

Senior management in large professional firms have great difficulty in communicating to the staff just what the vision or objectives for the firm are. Often when I ask people what their firm's objective for the year is they have no idea. And that's not good. Professional firms will often rely on a mission statement and a set of values on the website which never change as being the "rallying call", the reason for being for everyone in the company.

A problem is that company owners will probably say that the company's goal is to maximise profits, i.e. to maximise the amount of money paid to the shareholders at the end of the year. Conflicts arise in that the more money you pay to the staff the less there'll be for the shareholders. You might have a goal to "provide the best service at the lowest price". There's less conflict there because if you can achieve that you're probably maximising profits as a direct result. There's a balance to be struck. I strongly believe that every organisation should have a clearly understood objective and for each year. There may be supporting objectives at departmental and personal levels. Everyone must be made aware of how the firm is doing in meeting its objectives. The alternative, which is quite common, is to have a large group of employees working in a vacuum, which becomes a rut, where they feel less and less connection and commitment to the business and where their work and creative input will suffer.

A practical problem is that the leaders who are the most senior people in the company are usually the oldest and the longer you go on each year starts to feel like all the others. But most of the staff are younger, full of enthusiasm, new resolutions and hope for the New Year ahead and that energy will be dissipated if there's no passion, excitement and goal-setting coming from the leaders.

Avoid communicating by e-mail where possible especially if you are finding fault with anyone or any group. E-mails have no 'tone' and can be read differently by various people. People hate seeing any possible criticism of their work in writing and copied to others. A quick fair and direct chat is far better.

If possible make any company announcements which are sensitive by telling people and using noticeboards. E-mails are very easily forwarded by staff to their friends in other companies or the media.

LEADERS ARE WELL ORGANISED

Good leaders must be well organised. A leader who is working flat-out with passion, energy and commitment but who is jumping around like a headless chicken, is not providing great leadership. Being organised is one thing I was fairly good at. I like a tidy desk and I could never work from a desk piled high in paper, late for everything and always under pressure. A tip I learned at a time management seminar was to have just two folders on your desk. One is labelled "Must be done today." The other is labelled "Need not be done today." It's a simple system that I've used for years.

The golden rule for working effectively is to always tackle the most important thing first. Avoid procrastination. Avoid the temptation to do the easy things first – otherwise the day or week will disappear and you will have achieved very little.

DIVIDE AND CONQUER

Another great tip for being organised is "divide and conquer" – that is separate different pieces of your work, clients' work, activities in your life etc into different filing sections. It will be much easier to find things and to work with a clearer head.

I never knew anyone who lived and worked rigidly by the time manager system – i.e. scientifically allocating your time for each day/week/month into meeting various priorities and goals. It's a good system and parts work for me. At its simplest level the grouping of contacts/phone numbers/addresses etc., into sections called, for example, "Work", "Accounts", "Family", "Car", "Household Workmen", etc, has stood the test of time. After 25 years of diary systems, Customer Relationship Management Systems, IT databases and intranet contact systems the failsafe place to quickly find contact information and important memos that I needed was the ancient filofax on the bookshelf in my office with contacts listed per activity in my life. Divide and Conquer!

DELEGATE

Effective leaders delegate well: Delegation or the lack of it remains one of the biggest problems in organisations. There is often a misplaced but genuine desire among businesspeople to do the very best job possible for the client but which they believe can only be achieved by doing it themselves. Often wrong. I was slow to see the light on this myself but eventually became reasonably good at it I think. Many of us frequently find massive pressure of work and stress building up in the last few days before the two week summer holidays. Lots of work has been promised to be done, there are letters to write and clients to meet. Some work is already overdue.

The clients will be going on holiday too and we just can't miss the deadline and leave the work for another fortnight. In my earlier days I would eventually be forced to give a piece of work to an assistant or my secretary and go on holiday worried about what would happen. And guess what? On return from holiday you find that the letter went out, the client was met and the calls were made. And everything's just fine; there was no need for panic. We should be delegating every day and not just because we're going on holidays.

Any leader should be mentoring and bringing on people around him who are capable of handling routine work. Part of a leader's skill is judging just when and how to judiciously involve themselves in operational matters and when to provide their strategic/creative input in assisting and mentoring a junior. Good delegation is a win/win/win. The client gets their work done on time. Your assistant gets a boost from being entrusted to carry out some work for you and gains experience. You get an easier life and more time for strategic work. Win/win/win.

EMOTIONAL INTELLIGENCE

You will often hear leaders referred to as a good "people person". One strong characteristic of great leaders in business is their social skills. They turn contacts into relationships into friends. They have an empathy and an interest in people which others describe as charismatic. You need these qualities as leader both to inspire your followers/colleagues and to win business. You can become more charismatic by taking just a little more time to listen to others, remember people's names and snippets from their family life.

When you are speaking to someone, however briefly, give them the respect of your full concentration and maintain eye contact. There is nothing more off-putting than someone who won't look you in the eye or who is constantly looking past you to see who else is in the room. A smiling friendly expression is a lot more charismatic than a dour scowling one. I have also noticed that people referred to as 'charismatic' are usually great hosts. No matter how senior they are comfortable hosting and entertaining people, comfortable in company and in introducing people to each other. They are often first to pour the tea, hand around the plates or take someone's coat. Do more of these things.

TRUST YOUR INSTINCTS

If you're newly in a leadership role you can be reluctant to take radical action for fear of causing damage elsewhere with clients or colleagues. Just because things were always like this doesn't mean they should stay this way. If your gut instinct is telling you that something important is seriously wrong then take action to sort out that problem. Your colleagues have asked you to lead because they trust your judgement and experience. You must trust yourself. With experience you will probably find that that issue will cause you far more trouble in the long run if you ignore it, or opt for a half-hearted solution.

EFFECTIVENESS

The best leaders are *effective*. They find the right balance between listening to other's opinions and taking action to get things done. A leader who fiddles around too long seeking too many opinions will be ineffective. But a leader who makes radical changes over the heads of others without having considered their views will be a ruler and not a leader.

Your own effectiveness is crucial but I think an important challenge for a leader is to make sure that his organisation is effective; particularly for a large organisation. Many organisations develop a traditional hierarchy of departments, systems, consultation and working in teams, but is it effective? Is the output for the customers greater than the amount of time and money being put into creating that output? The more I work with organisations, particularly large ones, the more convinced I become that a lot of time and money is wasted in unnecessary meetings and consultations, with resulting communication problems.

The problem with always creating teams to tackle projects is that the larger the group the more likely there will be communications problems. Worst of all there is a dilution of responsibility for the end result. You are far better off having as small a number of people responsible for outcomes as possible. Let them delegate as appropriate but keep one person clearly responsible. The old maxim "too many cooks spoil the broth" applies.

A sad but good example of this occurred recently when a seriously ill Irish teenager was on the waiting list for an urgently required organ transplant. A call came through from a hospital in London that a suitable organ was available. There was enough time for a 12-year-old child with their mobile phone to arrange to send the sick girl by bus to Dublin Airport from where she could have got on any scheduled flight to London and then got a taxi to the hospital for the operation.

Instead, all of the teams involved swung into action to arrange a flight to London. There was the Health Authority, the hospital in Dublin, an agency charged with arranging air transportation for emergency medical cases, the AirCorps and the Coastguard helicopter service. Between them over a period of hours involving dozens of phone calls they made a complete mess of the situation and the unfortunate patient was eventually rushed to an airfield to be met by an aircraft which could not get her to London without re-fuelling and in time for the operation. The poor girl was stopped from travelling and missed the transplant. (Luckily, a few months later she received another organ and is recovering well). An inquiry was held and I can't remember who was held responsible – but that's the point. There were too many people, all well meaning, highly-trained and laden down with manuals, computers and communication equipment. Many large organisations have similar inefficiencies with overstaffing at middle management level with even more senior managers required to manage all the middle managers.

This is all usually at the cost of the frontline staff who have the greatest direct benefit to the customers. The cost of the inputs is far higher than the resulting benefit to the consumer. This is a real challenge for a leader to identify and break-up this culture. Classic symptoms of this culture of middle-management and empire building are too many meetings, meetings about meetings, a culture of ass-covering by unnecessarily copying e-mails to lots of people, lots of fancy job titles, too many offices/locations and lots of management car parking in the best spaces.

MAN THAT DOOR

A small tip for leaders is that when your company is holding some type of event or social gathering you should be positioned at the door both to welcome your guests and to say goodbye. I know this means staying by the door most of the night and it's hard work but I think it's worth the effort. Put out of your head any notion that this is demeaning or should be done by a secretary. You are the face of the company. Your clients and other clients of your colleagues will appreciate meeting the leader of the firm handling his business. In a crowded room he/she may not have the opportunity to approach you or to be introduced. You should make sure you meet everyone, you are a figurehead for your firm and you should be meeting the clients personally.

This method also means you won't get stuck with one client for too long. To avoid any embarrassment where you know a face but can't remember the name try standing just inside the door or a few feet behind and have your welcoming staff primed to say loudly as they hand over a name badge: "Now, there you are Mr Murphy or Ms O'Kelly."

BORN TO LEAD

To summarise – I don't know whether leaders are born or made. If there's no genetic component then there certainly is a very strong influence in a child's early years; just look at the huge proportion of leaders who are the first born in their families. A memorable insight from the London Business School occurred within the first few minutes of the introductory session. The attendance was approximately 80 leaders, or soon to be appointed leaders of organisations. There were heads of companies, colleges, charities and two MEPs from different regions around the world. The lecturer asked for everyone in the room, who was the first born child in their family to put up their hand.

Approximately 60 out of 80 people put up their hands. The lecturer did a count and said that this phenomenon was entirely in keeping with their findings over decades. The colleges explanation for this is that the first born child gets hot-housed and showered with 100 per cent of the undivided attention of his/her parents, in their crucial early years. Baby number two can never get the same level of attention and baby three gets even less. When the children start to play together it's always the firstborn who decides what game to play. And guess who makes up all the rules? The firstborn. The firstborn gets a headstart in life, is treated as special and quickly learns to exercise authority to influence and lead others. It's interesting, isn't it? One of the lessons I think is to make sure that all of our children feel special.

I have set out what I believe are the most important qualities for a leader in business. Many of them will come naturally to you; others you may need to work on. But the most important starting point is that you have a good awareness of your own strengths and weaknesses. And a last quotation by Peter Drucker, which is worth remembering:

"Management is doing things right;
Leadership is doing the right things."

// CHAPTER 13 //
GREAT SALESPEOPLE

Well, are great salesmen born or trained? In my view the very best salespeople I have seen were born that way. Because great selling comes naturally to the best salespeople, which once again brings us back to personality. The best salespeople will outsell others on any product or service; that's because their customer or client is buying the salesperson and not just the product or service. And yes, the best salespeople are Canaries too. That's not to say that we can't greatly improve the selling skills of the average salesperson with some training and insights because we certainly can. Here are some observations:

1. The most effective, powerful and successful salespeople believe in the product or service they are selling and are enthusiastic about it, (There's that enthusiasm factor again). It is a very compelling sales proposition when the salesperson obviously totally believes in what they are saying. It's very easy to spot a salesperson who is faking their belief in their offering and that is very off-putting. Make sure you've got the right salespeople selling the right products and services.

It's a hugely powerful selling influence if the salesperson has already bought the product or service. A few years ago I was going through the dreaded process of buying a new mobile phone in a Vodafone store. The usual bewildering array of phones tied to the wall with cables and nowhere to sit down. I was served by a really likeable young salesman. He talked me through a bewildering barrage of technical specifications, gigabytes, pixels and bundles, for all the different phones – he was clearly an expert. Eventually, I managed to narrow the choice down to three or four models.

"To be honest," he said, taking a phone out of his pocket, "this is the one I use myself. It's brilliant, I just love it."

Hallelujah! That made the decision easy for me and that's the one I bought. On one level I was buying a phone but what I really bought was his expert enthusiasm for a phone he used himself.

On a higher level but on the same principle, I once saw an ex-colleague of mine, Ronan O'Driscoll, who is an expert in property and a great salesman, sell four partly built apartments in a tower block in Toronto, over a lunch in Dublin. That's four sales, totalling about €1.5m.

Somehow the lunch conversation came around to buying overseas property (looking back, Ronan may have led that). Ronan was recommending investing in Toronto. He is known as an expert on overseas investment and he spoke knowledgeably about the Canadian economy and the Toronto market. He had visited the site and he trusted the developers. And, he had bought one of the apartments himself.

Four people at the table bought apartments – I know, because I was one of them. And Ronan was right. Despite most world markets crashing, the Toronto market was the place to be and we all made a profit. That's why co-investment has become popular, where companies selling, investing in or managing products actually take a small equity stake – also known as "putting your money where your mouth is". It's quite convincing when companies do it and it's really powerful when an individual commits personally.

2. Great salespeople are selling themselves. They listen more than they talk and they help their customer to buy. They assist them through the process and lead them to the conclusion.

3. Great salespeople develop long-term relationships. They become friends or trusted advisors to their customers to the point where their customers would never dream of buying elsewhere. That's real selling. For example, the very best car salesmen are sure of a sale every time their customer changes his car. Their customer is buying *them*, the salesman, not the car. The great salesman sells his care of the customer. The customer trusts that salesman and knows that if anything ever goes wrong with their car their salesman will solve the problem. There's usually also a bit of fun and ceremony attached to the purchase each time. That customer then influences their family to buy their cars there too – so the great salesman becomes the family car supplier. For ever. Great salesmen never abuse that trust, never let their customer down, keep in touch and never take the relationship for granted. Great salespeople nurture family loyalty and the strength of recommendations and word of mouth.

(I know a family in Dun Laoghaire, with five adult children, some now with their own children. They drive past many shoe repair shops to bring their shoes to a cobblers in Bray. Their late father used to bring his shoes there and spoke highly of the cobbler. The cobbler speaks highly of their late father. That's a lot of pairs of shoes to be repaired and they wouldn't dream of going anywhere else. That would be betraying a family tradition. Funny, isn't it? But very common. That's why lots of families have a 'family' doctor, solicitor, butcher, auctioneer, mechanic, gardener, insurance broker, builder etc – often for generations). Never underestimate the power of family loyalty and tradition.

4. Great salespeople filter what they say to be most effective for different customers. For a start, you'll only get so much time to try to move the sale forward. If you say too much the prospective buyer won't remember most of what you said. So, make every line count.

Start by thinking about your prospective buyer; who they are, where they're from, what their motivation is in considering this purchase. Use any information you can get either in advance or by asking "open questions". Now tailor your sales pitch to meet their requirements.

For example, when I was a young salesman selling a new industrial property, the first viewing would usually be done by the managing director of a company, sometimes accompanied by a head of sales/marketing. Both would probably be driving BMWs or Mercedes. The marketing person would be driving the coupe model. In selling to these people you mention the good value but talk about the company acquiring a "signature building" (never a unit) and making a statement in their marketplace. Emphasise the high profile of the building and the signage opportunities onto the main road. Talk about how impressed the companies customers will be with the beautiful showrooms. And make sure a lot of the conversation takes place in the managing director's potential new larger office, emphasising the en-suite shower/toilet. If your sales pitch goes well they'll send along the Financial Controller to look at the building a day or so later. He'll arrive in a Volvo. He's probably worried that the MD and Sales Director are over ambitious in their expansion plans and wonders if they can risk buying this building. Now you're talking about the fact that the building is new, isn't yet rated, and that they'll probably save two years rates. You also make reference to the new high-level insulation which will reduce future heating bills by 30 per cent. You also emphasise that this is a modern construction with full alarm and on-site security which will result in reduced insurance premiums. The service charge too on the estate is 25 per cent lower than where he is now. Don't tell him the other stuff; just land your punches. Even though it's the same product being sold to the same company you must tailor your pitch to suit whoever you're talking to.

5. Sell benefits not features. Lots of companies don't do this and just list features. For example, don't say: "The boot has a carrying capacity of 480 litres." Instead, say: "The enormous boot can easily take three large suitcases, and your golf bags, enough for any family holiday." Don't say: "Ample gardens with spectacular views over the bay", instead say: "Picture yourself relaxing in the beautiful gardens after a day's work, sipping a chilled white wine, as you feast your eyes on the spectacular view over the bay."

So, don't just list the features. Bring them to life for your purchaser by helping them visualise the benefits to them..

6. Stop talking. A really common mistake among inexperienced salespeople is to bring their customer to the point of buying. The customer may have already said "okay I'll take that one", or "Yep, that looks like the one for me." But our over-enthusiastic salesperson misses their cue to close the deal and introduces yet another choice/model/variation/option to the customer. The customer gets more confused and leaves "to think about it". You'd be amazed at how often this happens. Learn when to zip it.

7. Streetsmarts! In professional services where the transaction or selling process can continue over weeks or months, great salespeople have an instinct for sensing when the deal is NOT going to happen. Even though the purchaser and everyone advising him, on the face of it still seem to be going through the right motions, deeper down something has changed. The great salesperson instinctively senses this change in momentum and can usually predict which sales will fall through. Now, instead of wasting more of their own (and their client's time and money) on 'flogging a dead horse', they bring matters to a head and either force the sale through while there's still some hope or more likely, move on and sell to someone else. This 'street savvy' is not all that common. Canary salesmen have it because they learnt their lesson the first couple of times this happened to them and never forgot. But many, even senior and quite successful salespeople, never fully develop this instinct and naively go on believing in delaying tactics.

8. Create scarcity: Good salespeople in appropriate situations know when to create a "scarcity factor". They don't let their customer/client assume that there's an endless supply of the product or service at this price. Offers of goods or services at particular prices or fees should be linked to a time deadline. "We can take on three more clients at this fee before the tax return deadline." Or: "We can do your work at a special reduced fee, after the tax deadline – in our short quiet period." Create a little scarcity value and a lever on the customer to get on and do the deal.

9. Selling tactics work. Great salespeople think out their approach. There was a good example of this on a recent series of the television programme, 'The Apprentice' in Ireland. They were down to the last few contestants. The candidates were split into three teams – one headed by Steve Rayner, the eventual winner, who had already shown real selling skills. Each team was given cases of a medical product – a strip for sticking across your nose to improve breathing and already popular with some sports stars. Each team was given a territory and a list of pharmacies and sports facilities. The rules were simple: They could offer a discount of 33 per cent and whoever sold the most cases was the winner. The first two teams were shown on their selling visits, putting on good professional sales pitches and securing sales less a 33 per cent discount. The first team finished having sold seven cases. The second team finished having sold eleven cases. Steve Rayner had sold 65 cases. His approach? While his competitors offered a 33 per cent discount off the price of a case, Steve offered a "3 for 2" deal. "If you buy two cases today, I'll give you one extra case free." That's the same as a 33 per cent discount. So, always think about your approach in advance and find a little lever to motivate your buyer. "If you buy two cases today, I'll give you an extra case free."

10. Make it easy to buy. The hard part is achieving the sale; don't make it hard for your purchaser to do the deal. Sometimes retailers/vendors put purchasers off by over-complicating the buying process with too many questions, forms, or pieces of paper. Recently, I responded to a "Linked-In" invitation to attend a motivational and sales training day at Bill Cullen's Europa Training Academy. Bill Cullen (whom I admire) was to do a motivational piece and there were other good speakers. Always keen to learn I decided I would like to attend. As promised I got a call back and found myself talking to one of Bill's Apprentice winners. I had my credit card out ready to pay. But then they told me they would e-mail me the booking form. This turned out to be an excel spreadsheet on which I was to fill out my credit card details and return electronically. I couldn't get it to work and gave up in frustration. A few days later my computer broke and went in for repair. As of now I can't remember the date for the seminar and as I've no computer, I don't know if I'll attend. My money should have been in Bill's bank account weeks ago and the sale "in the bag". They should have taken credit card details over the phone. I don't think Bill would approve if he heard. So for goodness sake make the buying process easy.

11. Seize the moment: Great salespeople seize the moment. Many purchases, particularly the bigger ones – 'houses, cars, expensive clothes and financial products', are very dependent on the buyers mood at the time and that can change very quickly. If you can't get the deal closed now for some reason take a deposit or get some type of commitment as quickly as possible.

If you're in professional services and you've just had a positive meeting with a prospective client try to confirm your instructions "on the spot". Ideally get a signature on a note you've prepared detailing fees etc or at least get a verbal confirmation to go ahead immediately with some part of the work. This in itself creates a contract and you're much more likely to end up with the full instructions. A huge amount of business is lost by agreeing or offering to send a follow up letter summarising the advice you've already given, confirming your fees and detailed terms of engagement.

However, it usually takes a day or two to get the letter out and the prospective client may not read it for a couple of days. Over those few days the client's mood changes or one of his partners suggests someone else for the job. Every day that passes the impact of your great meeting diminishes. Try really hard not to leave a good pitch on the basis that you'll send a follow up letter. Don't be afraid at a meeting to "ask for the business" on the spot. You'll be surprised how many people say 'yes'. Agree your fees and leave on the understanding that you'll start the work immediately. Now you've created a contract. Start the work and by all means follow up with a letter containing details of your engagement. You are now confirming the instructions you've already been given and acted on rather than sending in a 'coldish' letter after the client has had time to change his mind several times over.

I've been unhappy with the service I was getting from a financial institution for some time and not sure what to do. Eventually I got all the files out and attended a good presentation by another bank. I liked them, understood them and I was in the mood to move my business. They said they would send me a written proposal. That was about three weeks ago. About a week ago I got an e-mail asking for my home address "as they were finalising the proposal". (My address was in the telephone book). Three weeks later nothing has arrived. My mood has changed several times in the interim. And they're not looking as efficient as they suggested in the meeting. Seize the moment. When your customer is 'on the hook' reel him in fast.

12. Integrity: Lastly, great salespeople have integrity; a pride in themselves and in what they are selling. Great salespeople know that they are in a long term game and they won't compromise their reputation and integrity for a 'quick buck' or a short term gain. Set a very high standard of integrity for yourself and guard your reputation fiercely because your reputation is everything and all that you have.

// CHAPTER 14 //
PROFESSIONAL SERVICES

The main difference between businesses that provide professional services e.g. solicitors, accountants, estate agents, brokers, etc, and more 'retail' type businesses is that professionals need to form even deeper and longer lasting relationships with their clients.

Whatever sector you're in write down the name of your own firm. Now write down the names of your main competitors. Consider what type of business or industry you are. You are classified as being in the "service sector" or the "service industry". Which of the firms that you have listed provides the best service? When I pose this question to a group from a firm there's usually no clear answer.

Isn't that surprising! Here's a group of people, studying, training and working for years in a particular service sector and from a small list of their competitors no-one really knows or agrees on who clearly provides the best service. In reality, some of your clients probably know best. If they've had occasion to use the services of a few of your competitors they'll have formed an opinion on who's best. Why not ask them what they think and why?

If we focus in a little closer you'll often find that clients view certain firms as being the best in some service areas but weaker in others. That's inevitably down to the individual people working in those areas. Once again we're straight back to the quality of your people and their personalities, how they behave at those crucial 'Canary Alert' moments and their ability to nurture and develop relationships with clients. The goal is to turn your business contacts and clients into friends. You must try and turn sterile professional relationships into friendships. Your friends are always going to be loyal. Your friends will always try and give you their business and they'll encourage other people to give you their business too.

Step back again for a moment and recall from earlier chapters how you and your firm look just like your competitors. The reason is probably because you *are* similar to your competitors. By definition, *most* of the firms in any sector provide the *average* service. The opportunity is for you to take those few small steps of improvement to become the outstanding firm.

BRAIN SPLIT

I want you to remember that you must approach every job with two different halves of your brain. The first half is your professional part, your experience, intelligence and ability to provide the required professional advice or to write that report. Unfortunately, you're not going to create any great new value with that because that's what your client is paying you for. That's what he expects. You are providing technical advice for the routine fee. Your competitors provide exactly the same service for a similar fee. As you have to do that type of work over and over again in order to become an expert it can eventually become routine and boring.

However, the other half of the job can be more fun – challenging, but more creative. This is where you need the other half of your brain to work out how to start moving that relationship away from just a professional one and closer to friendship. How can you up every aspect of the service you provide in doing this job so that the client experiences a real wow factor that makes him look forward to being involved with you again?

And it won't be your mere technical ability that will make an impact on your client. This is where you start using your personality and enthusiasm to help you stand out. This part of your job is the key to rising to the top of your profession and increasing your earning power. As Dale Carnegie wrote: "One can hire mere technical ability in engineering, accountancy, architecture, or any other profession at nominal salaries. But the person who has technical knowledge plus the ability to express ideas, to assume leadership and to arouse enthusiasm among people – that person is headed for higher earning power."

And as John D. Rockefeller was quoted in his heyday: "The ability to deal with people is as purchasable a commodity as sugar or coffee. And I will pay more for that ability, than for any other under the sun."

Strengthening a relationship with a client starts with small steps of personal touches. Develop an interest in your client's interests. Let your client do most of the talking. The more they talk, the more interesting they'll think that you are. You are gradually moving them to a position where your relationship becomes more important than the piece of work at hand. The test of whether or not you have succeeded in 'personalising' the relationship comes when one of you moves to another employer. Does the relationship continue as before and the routine work between you flows naturally despite the changed circumstances? If so, you have succeeded in 'personalising' the relationship above and beyond your 'work'. Your personal relationship is now more important than where you work. This is the Holy Grail.

You are not setting out to turn your clients into intensely close personal friends where you share deep emotional confidences (although some of these will develop). You are sincerely taking a stronger interest in your client as a person and allowing a comfortable friendship to develop over time where there is a mutual respect and trust and an unspoken understanding that your relationship is more than just a job.

Take those few extra seconds to chat about the match, the economy or something topical. Get to know your client and signal that your relationship will have a personal connection, apart from the technical work. It will happen gradually and naturally.

Once again, it will be combining excellence on a whole series of 'Small Steps', that will add up to you quickly convincing your client that you are outstanding. For example, how quickly do you return telephone calls? The usual objective in most professions is to return calls on the same day. Why not up your game and return calls quicker than your colleagues and competitors? With today's technology it's very easy to see your e-mails and phone messages from anywhere outside the office. Leave return messages even if it's outside of business hours. If you have an early meeting again the next morning leave a message on your client's phone or e-mail: "I'm sorry I missed you when I called back last night. I'm going into a meeting now but I'll call you at 10.30."

And do.

If you get into a habit of this you will stand out. If you can't return a call on the same day due to meetings, ensure that a colleague is charged with checking your messages and returning that call on the same day. Many of your competitors are sloppy about returning calls and often have "out of date" voicemails or e-mail notifications on their computer. This drives clients mad. Those professionals quickly get a reputation as hard to contact, unresponsive or slow. If you are routinely excellent at this you gain a reputation of being faster, sharper, and more interested in your clients. Every now and then your client will have a problem which is urgent to him. Who will he ring – the person who is hard to get or you that always responds to him? You, of course.

If a report, a letter or some work from you would reasonably be expected in three days then have it back in good time and preferably early. Clients love a solicitor who responds that little bit quicker, is efficient and easy to contact. They stand out a mile. It's Canary behaviour and it probably doesn't mean you have to work a whole lot harder. Just a little to be outstanding.

My grandfather Jim Connolly had another great piece of advice: "No matter what your job is always be at your desk 10 minutes earlier than expected and you'll stick out like a sore thumb." He's right again of course. That 10 minutes is nothing out of your day but it gives you time to think, get organised, react to events quicker than others; it sends all the right signals around the office.

If you can combine that little extra effort for your clients in your routine work with developing those clients as friends you will be outstanding. You will shoot to the top.

Over time find out about your client's interests, hobbies and family. Keep a record of their families' names, ages and schools etc. You should know where your client lives. Rather than e-mailing or posting a document maybe you could offer to drop it in yourself as you're passing on the way home? Suggest meeting up for a coffee or lunch. Routinely meet people for coffee/tea outside both of your offices. Develop the relationship into social invitations, dinners, theatre, golf – even better with relatively small numbers involved. Be very thankful if you have a domestic partner who will support you in this.

HAVE A PARTY

The most effective way to totally change the dynamic of your relationship with clients and contacts is to invite them to a party in your home. This is mostly done by the most senior and successful business leaders because they've seen how effective it is. The crucial point is that it's in your home; that's what takes the whole relationship 'out of the office' and into 'friendship'. You don't have to be living in a castle to do this. You can have drinks and finger food for a couple of hours, say 6-8pm on a Saturday which people can attend on their way to another event. You can have a barbeque. You can have parties surrounding sports events, national holidays etc, or an afternoon kids' event with facepainters. Maybe get caterers to help but try to keep it "homely". No corporate stuff and no goody bags. If it's big enough to have caterers ask them to dress down smartly – there's nothing worse in a house than fawning waiters in tuxedos making people feel uneasy.

You'll need a very supportive and understanding domestic partner because it's a big imposition but you can sprinkle in some other friends too as appropriate which makes it feel less like work. One big house party a year is hugely efficient and cost-effective. Time the invitation right so that you're inviting people whom you've got to know – not just raw contacts you've made in the last few days. Normally only half or so of the people you invite can attend but you'll still get great kudos from those you invited but couldn't come. You are clearly signalling that you are open to letting your professional connection develop into a level of friendship. The vast majority of clients will respond positively. As some invitees decline you keep issuing more invitations to get the optimum attendance. Don't keep inviting the same people and also invite colleagues as appropriate to the clients attending. Don't do any selling or pushing. As guests leave they'll usually be saying: "We must have lunch/a coffee/ play golf/meet for a chat/keep in touch", etc. You make sure you do that follow-up. Their door will be wide open. You're on a real winner if your client's partner has enjoyed himself/herself and is making social arrangements with your partner. Always generously thank and appreciate your partner for their part in transforming your career. I always encourage companies to make an allowance available to staff for holding house parties. Everyone knows this makes sense, but it's hard work as it infringes on your "time-off" and very few people make the effort to do it. If you hold one large house party a year and say six dinner parties for smaller numbers of key clients you will transform your winning of business and your career.

So, let's get the party started!

I've had great fun and success throwing parties at my house over the years, and a bit of creativity goes a long way. The centrepiece for my parties is "The Old Longhill Bar". This is a spare room which I had converted to replicate a country pub. A good carpenter made the bar cheaply enough. After that all it needed was a few old mirrors, barstools, an old pool table and old beer pumps and coolers which a pub was throwing out. The walls of the bar are covered in dozens of signed sports jerseys, photographs, memorabilia and autographs which I have collected over the years. It's a really interesting room.

I started having an annual party centred on the bar and the theme was that everyone invited had to bring an autograph from someone famous. The most famous autograph would win a prize and the winners were announced by me with much fanfare wearing an ancient tuxedo. The prize for the winner was a plastic 'Oscar' and a voucher for free drink in the bar for 100 years. Pure fun and games. Every year, I would produce a surprise 'special guest' entertainer to perform. The first year I wrote to Ronnie Drew. He wasn't too busy and readily agreed to perform in the bar. You could have cut the atmosphere with a knife as the crowd packed into this little 'country bar' and were enthralled as Ronnie regaled us with songs and drinking stories. Ronnie was so good that I asked him back for the next year. Hazel O'Connor, a huge star from the eighties lives in Wicklow, so I wrote to her and she also agreed to perform. She arrived in that year with Cormac De Barra, a gifted traditional musician, who plays an old Irish Harp. Hazel had just won a prize at the Edinburgh Theatre Festival for her play, which is a re-enactment of her life story. She uses puppets to represent her solicitor, manager, and accountant and throughout she sang her biggest hits.

It was incredible. The hairs were standing up on the back of our necks. On another occasion, I wrote a polite letter to Chris De Burgh who had moved to the area and offered a decent donation to a charity if he would like to be our guest performer. He enthusiastically arrived along with his wife Diane and it was good fun to be able to introduce some "local, up and coming talent". Chris's one or two songs turned into a full-on concert to 40 or 50 people packed three deep into the bar. These were all hugely memorable experiences for everyone attending.

STRENGTHEN THE PERSONAL RELATIONSHIP

Once you've signalled to your client, (and they've responded) that this professional relationship is moving into friendship territory, keep looking for ways to keep strengthening it. It's hard to score points around the job you're doing for him because he expects that to be excellent. You must really jump on opportunities to help them personally. Giving a gift is very powerful when appropriate as the recipient feels pleased but also instinctively feels a need to reciprocate. Don't get this crassly wrong. I know a chief executive of a plc who met a professional at a social function for the first time coming up to Christmas. They exchanged cards. When he got home from work the next evening on his doorstep was an enormous expensive hamper packed with fine wines and salmon from the man he had just met. The chief executive was appalled and thought this was amateurish and verging on attempted bribery. The hamper was sent back with a polite note declining acceptance. The man who sent the hamper had set his company back years in the eyes of an influential businessman and will never get business from that plc.

I have found that a gift of a book is very effective. It is low cost but can have a very high value to someone. Look for opportunities in conversations where your client shows interest in a topic, a business or economic issue perhaps. You should be well-read and familiar with several notable books. You just slip into the conversation that "such and such author" is very interesting or controversial on that. I must lend you my copy."

"Great," says your client – expecting you to forget. It's then nicely effective when you drop in a new copy of the book with a personalised message. They'll never forget it and again you've signalled that this is more than just a cold, professional relationship. I had great success gifting clients with Malcolm Gladwell's 'The Tipping Point', or for controversy Naomi Klein's 'No Logo'. Books on the history of your city or location are always interesting.

You should on an ongoing basis look for opportunities to 'stand-out', to strengthen that personal connection and not just think about the routine job. Helping secure work experience for your client's children is hugely effective. A classic example for me involved a very good client called James Carroll, known as Jimmy, who permits me to tell this story:

Jimmy is a very successful businessman, property owner and investor in Dublin – well-known and very influential. Jimmy and I had become friends over 20 years of doing business and he was an advocate for me and my firm, regularly sending business our way. One lunchtime I was in the staff canteen when the phone rang. It was Jimmy looking for me. He was in a state of panic. He had come into town to bid on behalf of his daughter for a house that was up for auction at another estate agents. The auction was due to be held in 35 minutes and he had forgotten his cheque book and would be unable to pay a deposit as required. I kept him on the line, spoke with our company accountant and we quickly agreed that we would give Jimmy a blank company cheque which I delivered to him before the auction. He bought the house and, of course, sorted the cheque out the next day. Jimmy couldn't thank us enough for our trust in him and what we had done. He was at risk of his daughter missing out on her dream home. Jimmy changed gear and went from being an advocate for me and the firm into a full-time ambassador, sending very valuable business our way at every possible occasion. He says he will never forget our help that day.

Over the years clients became aware that I could sing and entertain. I would regularly be telephoned by clients to ask if I would bring the guitar to a Christmas party to which I was invited. Now a company's own party for its own clients or staff is very important to them. No matter how good the corporate entertainment is, it always makes a big difference if one of the partygoers gets up to sing and does a good job. I gladly agreed to all of these requests. It was totally natural for me – after a few beers I've sung at nearly every party I've been at. If invited though, I would be a bit more professional about preparing what I was going to do, such as namechecking a few important guests, liaising with the band in advance so that the backing was seamless and generally make sure that I added as much to that party as possible. I am happy to do so because it's always good fun and it's nice to help. I was mindful too that every song goldplated our bond to that client in a way that writing 20 reports could never do.

On another occasion I was driving with a client to some meeting. He became interested in my hand-controls and I demonstrated how they worked. He explained that he was worried about his mother's ability to drive following an illness. Someone had suggested hand controls but she was terrified at the idea and they knew nothing about them. I said that I had a portable set at home and I would happily explain them to his mother. The next weekend the client met me at his old family home. In 10 minutes I fitted the controls on to his mother's car and showed her how to use them. She ordered a set for herself and recommenced driving thus regaining her independence. She was delighted. My client was delighted. He gave me every piece of business he ever could for 20 years.

I would like to think that I would instinctively go out of my way to help anyone. But when you are spending time helping a client in a way which is disconnected from normal business, you are creating lifelong personal connections. We all have different talents and expertise which can help people. So never miss an opportunity to help out your client with something personal to them.

Routinely look for opportunities to source business for your clients and to introduce them to your contacts. You're scoring heavily when you're doing this. Another rich source of connections is parents of your children's friends at school and on sports teams. Some schools are now organising business networking forums for parents. Always keep your eyes and ears open. Always have a business card in your suit and jeans.

As your career develops your network of business contacts widens and deepens as more and more of them move closer to being your friends. You can introduce them to each other and in turn they'll be looking out for business opportunities for you. Your private network of contacts and friends becomes a powerful force propelling you upwards. Your network gives you 'leverage' in that it's working for you, promoting your personal brand and bringing you business all the time.

MAXIMISE CONTACT

The most successful business people I know in the world of professional services make sure to keep in very regular contact with their clients and others involved in any piece of work. You don't have to change your world to do this and it's easy enough to 'diary in' a time every week during which you can call your clients and keep in touch. Even if you're just leaving a message reporting that there are no developments, your client feels very well looked after. If you don't keep in regular contact you will find yourself missing out on pieces of news or information. If you wait too long, events will have moved on without you and you will lose control and become sidelined in the proceedings. Smart business people develop an instinct for making calls at times when something may have happened e.g. after your client has had a meeting. You must stay close to your clients and close to the action.

It can also be very effective to call a client when there is no particular reason to do so. It's friendly and often new leads or work can develop from the chat. I routinely devoted the last working day before Christmas to telephoning all my best clients. You would often get them in their office with time to spare. I was just calling to wish them a Happy Christmas but, because of the time of year, the conversation would usually wander into chats about family, holidays and plans for next year. I found that clients appreciated these calls and responded naturally. Try it.

A TIP

Make sure that any staff member leaving your organisation does so on the best possible friendly terms. They may be moving to a competitor or out of your industry but you'll be surprised at how many will crop up again years later in influential senior positions elsewhere. Many will become clients or can influence business towards you. Most people will retain a sense of loyalty and fondness for wherever they started out, providing you treated them well. They'll be motivated to help you out. It's a very good idea for any organisation to keep in touch with its "alumni". This can be easily enough achieved by keeping ex-staff on your mailing list for your publications and holding an annual get-together, ideally in the hostelry where they will have fond memories of celebrations in their youth. You'll be amazed how much business will come back to you by keeping in touch.

A TRUTH

In most organisations it's the business winners that rise quickest to the top. These are the Canaries, the can-do people who are good at retaining their clients and winning new clients as well as doing the routine professional work. Continuing my theme on 'leverage', this is where you should be looking at freeing those people up to do more of what they do best. They will add far more value for you bringing in business than they can ever do by billing out routine work. If you have an obvious Canary business winner, invest in putting in more support behind them to handle their routine work, and free them up to do what they do best.

TEAMWORK

People who are naturally outgoing, good at winning business and good at sales are invaluable. But their personality type and strengths may not be best suited to looking for fine detail or handling large amounts of routine work in a disciplined way that meets deadlines. Lots of other people are best at those things but don't feel comfortable trying to sell themselves. A successful team needs the right blend of both types of people and this is one of the great and interesting challenges of leadership. You must assemble your team so that you play your players in their best positions. Don't be afraid to make some changes. Moving some of your people around can inject new life into relationships for both clients and staff.

KEEP YOUR EXISTING CLIENTS FEELING SPECIAL

Don't let those long-standing relationships with your clients go stale. Just because they're not complaining doesn't mean they feel happy.

If long-standing clients begin to feel that you have become a bit complacent about their business they will be wide open to approaches from your competitors. Rest assured your competitors will make approaches. Sometimes a client will competitively tender a piece of work which you would normally expect to get. They're sending you a clear signal that they don't feel "loved" anymore. So you must keep close to your clients and regularly ask them for feedback on how you are doing. Far better to pick up any rumblings about complacency when you have time to rectify the situation. Keep making contact.

I read a survey the other day which said that about two-thirds of clients who change their service providers do so "for no particular reason". Apathy had set in. Never take your longstanding clients for granted. They are the "family silver".

I was chatting with a professional person in the past year. The subject of mobile phones came up:

Friend: "I'm going to leave O2."

Me: "Why?"

Friend: "They just never do anything for me."

Me: "Oh, well, are you happy with their charges? Do they drop calls?"

Friend: "No, that's all fine. But everyday I'm hearing other phone companies making all sorts of offers. And O2 never do anything for me."

My friend may have been wrong but that was her perception. Beware the client who is paying his fees, not complaining and who you think is happy. He may be about to move.

GET OUT AND MEET YOUR MARKET

It's essential that you find a good reason to meet the business givers and influencers in your market. Sending letters and mailshots is far less effective. One initiative I recall demonstrates this very clearly. By mid-2001, a mini commercial property boom largely driven by the dotcom sector was slowing rapidly and deals were becoming scarce. We were worried about the prospects for the next year. Then came the shocking tragedy of 9-11 and the second Gulf War.

The telephones stopped ringing and the markets were grinding to a halt. As one colleague drily suggested: "We may as well shut the doors for next year." There was a real risk of lay-offs. Faced with this adversity I was forced into some lateral thinking and I came up with a plan. If the economy was going to get as bad as we feared there would be a spate of insolvencies. My plan was to target the long forgotten insolvency experts – the receivers and liquidators.

During the 1980s insolvency was one of the busiest areas for the accountancy practices and several individuals became nationally known due to their appointment as receivers or liquidators to large companies. Throughout the better decade of the nineties insolvencies petered out and the insolvency experts almost became extinct. I sensed their rebirth and devised my plan of 'Small Steps'.

I knew none of the insolvency experts at that time and the firm had lost touch with them. Step one was to change that. I decided that we would offer a specialised insolvency service and I formed an alliance with a plant and machinery expert who specialised in selling the equipment in buildings. We could now offer a 'one stop shop' to the receivers/liquidators. We also offered a single invoice facility for our combined services. As receivers/liquidators are often appointed at short notice and become responsible for securing and maintaining buildings and equipment, I offered my property management colleagues 24 hour emergency telephone number for anyone needing security or technical help. I arranged for a firm of solicitors who were prominent in the insolvency area to come to our office and to brief our team on the latest insolvency legislation. All of this was pulled together in a glossy brochure. Time to hit the streets.

It was easy to identify the dozen or so leading insolvency practitioners and I did some basic research on each; their personality types, business alliances, where they lived, old schools, their interests etc, all looking for hooks. I had also learned that each bank that would appoint a liquidator/receiver had its own system for doing so but again there was usually one individual who had primary responsibility. It was important to get to know those individuals as well and to make sure they were well aware of our services. We set up an insolvency excel sheet packed with information on the receivers/liquidators and banking teams. We started calling them cold or approaching through contacts looking for a brief meeting to present our new, tailormade insolvency service. I had up to 15 meetings in the first fortnight and picked off the last few over the next week or two. I was in Chameleon mode. In all cases we were well received. If anything arose in the meeting I followed it up immediately. I referred some business contacts to the insolvency firms. We invited the insolvency experts and their second and third in command to various functions. We sent them our publications. I also sent our brochure to the leading lawyers in the insolvency area, further heightening awareness in the sector.

Within weeks a number of insolvencies started occurring and our phone started ringing. There was a particular meltdown in the IT sector and specifically in the area of 'server centres' or 'data hotels'. These were highly specialised and costly buildings which hosted servers for their client companies. They had drastically oversupplied the market and they started falling like ninepins. We were instructed to value and sell the first large server centre that failed. We had to get up to speed very quickly on this very specialised type of building and equipment and the likely buyers. We arranged a successful sale. When a liquidator was appointed to a second server centre we were in pole position for the job as we knew the market better than anyone. We got that job, too. And the third. And the fourth. From memory there were 10 insolvency instructions of data centres in a year and we were appointed on eight. We also won more than our fair share of instructions to handle insolvencies in a range of other sectors. In the first year of our "new" insolvency service we earned approximately €1.5m in fees. One fee alone was approximately €350,000, beautifully replacing the turnover which was being lost through the inactivity in the traditional sectors. There was a huge opportunity for everyone at the heart of a setback in the property markets.

Not one liquidator ever asked for a single invoice. No one ever rang our 24 hour emergency telephone number. No one ever quizzed us on a finer detail of insolvency law. We had sharpened up our act, polished up how we presented our normal professional service and crucially we had gone to see all the influential people in the market before anyone else. We were enthusiastic, hungry and professional. We made sure we were in the right place at the right time. Make sure you know and regularly meet the influential people in your market. Business will follow.

CONCLUSION

In a professional firm each individual must take responsibility for his own actions every day in nurturing and developing clients. The 'brand' and the acknowledged business winners can only do so much. Becoming a good business developer yourself is the fastest way to advance your career.

// CHAPTER 15 //
BEING BONO - LESSONS FROM SHOWBIZ

A while ago on the radio I heard Fr. Brian Darcy say how much he admired people in showbusiness. "Just think of the bravery and hard work it takes for someone to walk out on a stage, in front of a crowd, and to rely entirely on their talent as an actor or performer to hold their audience."

For the entertainer the audience is his customer and he is in the business of putting on a show. He's trying to make that show so memorable that his audience will come back for more. And tell all their friends to come too. Isn't that exactly what we are trying to achieve in business generally? When you are representing yourself or your organisation in business you should remember that you too are "on show". You are standing in the spotlight and you must make sure that you give your very best performance. As I suggested in the chapter on chameleons, you may be fine-tuning your performance to suit each audience but your goal is always to leave your audience delighted and coming back for more.

I've had great fun and rewards from singing professionally and writing music. My party piece Bono impersonation grew so popular that I was able to 'commercialise' it and create a Bono comedy character, known as "Hugh Toohy – The World's Greatest Rockstar" (see www.HughToohy.com).

"Being Bono" has brought me all over the world and I've performed in the US, South Africa and in parts of Europe. Bono's a hero of mine. He's also obviously a Canary – always trying new things, keen to learn, keen to help, enthusiastic, loyal to friends, with a huge sense of duty and a remarkable work ethic. He's a great example to younger people, especially.

The key to my Bono act is to make an instant 'fun' connection with the audience. I may look and sound like Bono, but so do other impersonators. To get the audience behind me I quickly let them know that I'm not taking this seriously by over-acting and hamming everything up, and with self-deprecating over the top props and 'silly' jokes. Once you've got the audience fully relaxed and clear about whatever you're doing, you're on a winner. They'll cheer even louder when things go wrong and mistakes as bad as a skipping backing track are assumed to be a hilarious part of the act. It's just the same in business, the first few seconds are when a vital impression is formed by establishing a friendly connection from the outset. Give them your biggest smile, a firm handshake and really strong eye contact. Take a few extra seconds to chat about the weather/the match/the economy – whatever. Now, you're building your foundations.

This principle is equally true for when you stand up in front of an audience to deliver a presentation or when you walk into a room for an interview. You must be very conscious of the need to transmit the right energy by making the right impression from the outset. You must work to establish that emotional connection with your audience even if the starting emotion is simply friendliness. Remember that you are 'on stage' from the moment you walk into that room and you are essentially delivering a rehearsed performance. Several times when serving on interview panels I have seen the energy completely sucked out of a room by the appearance, body language or demeanour of people. Their chances have evaporated before they even speak.

I've found that when you are addressing a large business group from a stage or lectern, especially when using a microphone, you need to speak a little more slowly and leave slightly longer gaps between points. Any pauses or gestures almost need to be over-emphasised as it takes longer for a large group to react. Often, the reaction, whether it is surprise, laughter or applause seems to ripple through a large audience like a wave.

A large audience almost develops an energy or personality of its own. It's hard to put your finger on it but you could deliver the same performance in the same room to similar people on three different nights and each audience will respond differently. Sometimes there will seem to be a better atmosphere than others and some audiences are referred to as better than others. Get a feel for your audience and make sure you leave enough time for them to take-in each point. Pacing of delivery is a real stagecraft and you'll improve with experience. Be mindful that sometimes there may be a tiny delay between the time when parts of the audience will hear you, depending on the quality of the PA system.

I learnt another valuable lesson from showbusiness from the time I sang and played with a rock band in the eighties and nineties. I concentrated on forming a friendly connection with the audience. I would remind the musicians to keep smiling and always look like we were having great fun. Throw in a bit of banter with the audience and they'll connect with you. There's nothing worse than seeing top wedding bands going through the motions, with a frantic frontman trying to get the audience going while the rest of the musicians look like they've just come from a funeral. Always show enthusiasm.

The band I played with then grew fairly popular, appeared on 'The Late Late Show' and played in many of the top Dublin venues. I was pleasantly surprised at how many big gigs we got – often more than some of the really top bands. Much of this was simply down to the way we maximized our interaction with the audience. I remember thanking the manager of a Dublin venue for the very generous number of gigs we were getting ahead of 'bigger' bands.

"That's because you're no trouble," he said.

"What do you mean?" I asked.

"Bloody musicians," he says, "unreliable. Never drop in the posters when they promise, someone's always late for the gig, late sound-checks, too loud and play on too long when I'm trying to close the place down."

"But," he smiled as he paid me for our gig. "You, are reliable. I get what I want."

So there it was. An early lesson that you can be more successful than competitors who may have greater abilities, simply by being reliable and consistently giving your clients what they want. "Most of success is down to turning up." So, be early, be reliable, and be consistent – many of your competitors won't be.

In 1994, the Irish soccer team qualified for the World Cup in the USA. I heard that a competition was being advertised with a great prize for whoever could write the best "Anthem" for the Irish World Cup players to sing. I enjoyed co-writing the song but with just one day to go we had to submit a CD recording to RTE. I believed in the song enough to hire a studio for an evening. I didn't have a band at the time and I needed six musicians including a fiddle player. With hours to go I picked my dream line up of musicians and began calling them. Every single one of them turned up that night, we made a great demo and won the competition. These were all musicians I had played with over the years. They knew that I could be taken seriously and whatever we had done before had always been successful. They believed that this song would be too even though there were hundreds of entries. Success breeds success.

As I delivered the CD to RTE the next day, I was 100 per cent certain that we would win. And we did. The song went straight to Number 1 in the charts and was only displaced by "Riverdance".

I earned a reputation as someone reliable who could produce novelty/comedy songs very quickly and I got several commissions from RTE to write and record pieces for various programmes.

I absorbed another lesson when watching the professionalism and detailed preparation which people at the top of their game put into their job. For a 30-minute interview on 'The Late Late Show', I was interviewed by a researcher three times, each time for two or three hours. He also met me for a night of drinking pints, (to see what I was like outside the office, I suppose), all before the interview was confirmed. For the performance by my band, 'The Late Late Show' booked a ballroom in a hotel in Bray for us to set-up and perform in. Two technical men arrived out, one for sound and one for cameras. They carefully checked all of our equipment, the leads, connections, amps etc. They then rolled out enormous sheets of paper on the dancefloor and asked us to play our song over and over again as they walked around on the paper in circles, drawing lines and arrows for the movements of cameras. On the afternoon of the show the musical acts rehearse again in the studio and there were all the cameras, swishing around following their diagrams as we played. And all for three minutes of live TV. That's professionalism.

Another memorable experience which showbusiness gave me was when I played at a wedding in Avoca. With my pal John Glynn on piano we performed as The John Paul Two and mixed-in plenty of comedy with our usual songs. A few days later I received a phone call from the late Dermot Morgan, aka Father Ted. He had been at the wedding and had enjoyed the show. "Any band called The John Paul Two, I have to be part of," he said. We met up a few nights later. At the time, his radio programme "Scrap Saturday" was hugely successful but Dermot was giving out about how little he was earning. He had a plan to put together a show which would be a mixture of comedy and music and he wanted us to join him. I was a big fan of Dermot's comedy and without thinking for a second about how on earth I would fit this alongside a busy day job, we agreed.

The plan was that we would meet in my apartment every Thursday to write songs and rehearse. The following few Thursdays were as chaotic and entertaining as I have known. To put it mildly, Dermot was not well organised. He was invariably at least an hour late. On the very first night, he arrived late and locked his keys into his car. There followed as funny an hour as I can remember in my life as a group of my neighbours gathered around his banger and tried to help as he stuck wire coat-hangers and screwdrivers into various holes in the car, cursing frantically as he morphed from Eamon Dunphy to CJ Haughey to P. Flynn.

What a performance.

The actual rehearsals weren't a whole lot more productive and most of the time was spent falling around the place laughing as Dermot switched from character to character. By the time we had three or four half-written songs, Father Ted was taking off and as Dermot said: "Yet another unfinished project."

I was half glad as I don't know how I could have managed to go on those extensive tours he was planning. Dermot would openly say that he was great at having brilliant ideas but not good at actually delivering his projects, and we all need to beware of that danger. He was a great character. It was so sad that he died so young and at the peak of his success.

In showbusiness the most successful people over time are the people that work and practise the hardest. The people at the very top of the tree are usually the friendliest and the most courteous and respectful to their fans. They know how hard they had to work to get where they are, they don't lose contact with their customers and they know that complacency means a downfall. We should remember that lesson in all our businesses because we are always on show. We must give our best performance every time. Success breeds success. The more success you have, the more people will believe in you and then success gets even easier.

// CHAPTER 16 //
COMPUTERS AND INFORMATION TECHNOLOGY

The business world runs on information technology but make sure it's improving life for your customer or client and not getting in the way. People aren't computers; they have emotions, don't think in straight lines and your organisation's processes may not be what your customer values. Here are a few common mistakes:

1. Talk to me – not the damn computer. An organisation spends a lot of time and money on a computer system and then trains its frontline staff how to use it. The staff are a bit nervous about it and worried that they'll make mistakes. The problem is that the computer and the process of putting information into boxes becomes the priority focus and the customer is forgotten. Classic examples include my car service centre. There are three or four service staff sitting behind computers. You walk up to the computer or hang around until someone says hello. You say you've brought your car in for the service; it's already booked in. Instead of shaking hands, greeting you enthusiastically and getting into chat, they ask you to sit down on your side of the counter and they then focus entirely on a long drawn out process of tapping keys and filling boxes.

Intermittently, you'll be asked your address or phone number. There's no attempt to chat to you or ask you "how's the car going" etc. There's little eye contact with you. Eventually they'll stand up and walk away from you without saying anything. It turns out they're going over to the printer where they wait while something prints out. The computer, the system, is the focus – they've lost sight of the customer.

Another example recently was when I brought my 82-year-old father to have a cataract removed at a top private hospital – which presents itself as a five star, top of the range facility. My father was terrified. On the drive there he turned to me and said: "You know, one in every 100 people having this done go blind." I tried to reassure him. We took the lift to the day treatment reception area where there were two or three receptionists.

When one became free my father took a seat in front of her while I observed. This receptionist knew from her system that my father was booked in for a procedure. She knew he was elderly, knew where he lived and could have guessed he would be nervous. The checking in started with my father clearly saying his name.

"James McNeive – N-E-I-V-E"

The receptionist looked at her screen and began tapping keys. Tap-tap. Tap-tap. Tap-tap-tap. More tap-tap. More tap-tap-tap. For several minutes without once looking at him. Eventually she said: "And your date of birth?"

"25th September 1928".

Tap –tap-tap. Tap-tap. Another long period of tapping. Then without saying anything she got up and walked away. She walked to the end of the counter and waited for something to print. Then she returned and told my father to go down to basement level for an eye examination and handed him a form. And that was it. Her sole focus was her computer and her determination to make sure she did that part of her job properly. But she forgot that part of her job is to welcome their patient – their customer. She made no attempt to put him at his ease with a little chat, didn't reassure him. Nothing. When we went for the eye test the receptionist there stood up.

"Oh, how are you Mr. McNeive?" A big smile and a handshake.

"I'm not too bad. A bit nervous to be honest."

"Oh, don't you worry, it's a very simple and routine procedure. Now, take a seat and we'll do the paperwork." Then, waving and smiling at me; "Oh and I see you've brought your chauffeur."

Everyone's laughing and smiling. She says to me: "Please take a seat, wherever you like. There's water over there and plenty of newspapers."

Then she steered my Dad through her part of the process and engaged with her computer after she'd done the best part of her work. What a difference. Same job. Same company. Same building. Same process. Very different outcome.

Another recent medical episode underlined my theory that competitors in any sector will generally settle at around the same level of customer service which they think is good enough, because everyone else is the same and they can get away with it. My son Killian broke his jaw in three places and damaged teeth while playing rugby. This disaster saw the VHI directing us to three different top of the range private hospitals over a few days. At the Hermitage Hospital the welcome was efficient but a little brusque. The Northbrook Clinic provided a warmer, friendlier welcome at the various departments. At the high tech modern hospital where Killian with a massively swollen jaw arrived nervously at 7am for a major operation, he received a sterile computer-tapping checking-in procedure, which was mostly concerned about the details of his health insurance and with no welcome or words of reassurance or pity whatsoever. The same thing happened for his second operation.

Just think about that. Just like my Dad's hospital they know exactly when a patient will arrive in for an operation. They know what the problem is. And they know he'll have been fasting, is weak, in pain and is nervous. Just imagine that you met someone on the street who had recently been injured in an accident and was facing surgery. You would sympathise with them, wish them well and reassure them. Yet in the very hospital which has all this information and is being paid for their service, the welcome has become purely a computer process and they have lost sight of their patient. The patient becomes a number and part of a process. Funny, isn't it? And after paying hundreds or thousands of euro for your consultation or operation, most new hospitals charge you a few more euro for the privilege of parking at their hospital. You leave feeling gouged. The process for Killian was largely recovered by a very empathetic nurse at the next stage.

So watch your own staff and make sure they haven't slipped into giving most of their attention to their computer. It's widespread.

2. Travelling: Every time I travel in America, I'm reminded of a variation of the above, that is, a concentration and fascination by staff on their process of checking guests in, especially in restaurants. You'll get a cheery welcome but once they've got your name, they're overpowered by a desire to enter it into their computer or find it already there.

"Ah yes, you have a reservation for two," (You knew that). They then concentrate on an often complicated process of printing out some ticket or voucher that has to be handed to the maitre'd, who in turn hands it to your server. This is all explained to you when all you want to do is sit down. The server then leaves the ticket on the table. They let the process get in the way of serving the customer. There's actually a surprising amount of bureaucracy and over-complication in business in the States.

Earlier this year, I spent several weeks in the US. I accumulated so much stuff that I needed to buy an extra large suitcase. I was in Sarasota, Florida, and a friend recommended I go to Kohl – who are an upmarket retailer with a big store at the Westfield Centre. "They're big on customer service and they give great discounts on luggage," I was told.

The store was enormous and very bright with big wide aisles. I found the luggage section where there was a huge range. Many of the cases weren't priced individually and the offer that day was that if you bought any piece you got any cheaper piece free. And there was another 15 per cent discount for over 60s. I was assisted by a very friendly manager. She asked where I was from and we chatted about Europe. I explained that I didn't want a second case and asked what deal I could get for a single, large case. Now the problems started. She had an electronic device around her neck which she ran over the barcodes and she started telling me individual prices. Then her gadget stopped working. She was embarrassed and we laughed and agreed how IT can often let you down. She called a colleague on her radio: "Mike, I'm here in luggage serving a guest. Can you bring me another price-reader please." They refer to their customers as "guests". Maybe a little over the top for Europe but when you think about it, if all your staff treated your customers as they would a 'guest' to their home, wouldn't the service be great? The replacement device worked fine and I chose a huge suitcase. Then I defeated the purpose of the visit by half-filling it with jackets and presents which were at fantastically low prices.

Back at the check-out, my friendly assistant returned to help. "Would you like to join our Customer's Club?" she asked. "You get 20 per cent discount on everything you've just bought and on anything you buy on the internet. "Great," I said, "Why not?"

When my case was scanned at the checkout a higher price came up causing more embarrassment and confusion. My assistant decided I must get the case at the lower price as that was what I was told. My bill was $440. Then I started the process of joining the Customer Club by tapping on a computer screen. Halfway through everything froze and calls had to be made to IT support. It turned out the system couldn't accept an Irish social security number. More embarrassment. After another consultation with her boss, my manager said they would give me the 20 per cent discount anyway as they had offered it. My case was carefully packed for me and my assistant walked me to the door and asked that: "You come back and visit us again sometime."

I certainly would.

This was a lovely store offering great value with a very strong customer service ethic. But at every stage the IT was getting in the way of the customer service. Make sure something similar isn't going on in your business, ideally by having some friends test the buying process from your company.

3. Customer Relationship Management (CRM): These systems are great but for goodness sake keep them simple or the system will never become part of routine working for staff. I know of relatively few CRM systems in large companies where everyone works them to their potential or as they were designed. I know of several executives who have lost their jobs and small fortunes trying to implement complicated CRM software systems.

Beware of allowing a fascination with processes and systems get in the way. I have objected to and watched aghast as a manufacturing company I know, part of a large international organisation, has spent about a year trying to adapt to a European centralised 'customer service' questionnaire process. (The form only allows a line or two for a client's views on anything) In the interim no-one is sitting down with the top clients and finding out whether they're happy or not.

4. Digital Media: Particularly among professional firms, I'm beginning to see some panic breaking out. "What the hell is all this digital marketing and social media stuff about – let's hope it goes away." If you haven't already done so you need to get up to speed quickly on this subject because it is not going away. Some of the large professional firms already have Facebook sites which become particularly active around graduate recruitment time. Most firms encourage their staff to join 'Linked-In' and other networks. I strongly urge you to make sure that you understand all these media and how they may or may not work for you. Write down a plan for what you're going to do. These new media are the growing forms of communication and if you ignore them you risk being left behind.

Traditional advertising and PR media are reducing in impact and increasingly fragmented newspaper and magazine circulation figures are dropping, as are most traditional TV and radio audiences. I need look no further than my own three teenage children as an example of the next generation of business owners and consumers: They don't buy or read newspapers and increasingly they watch their TV programmes on computer. They don't wear watches. They don't use phone books. They don't use the Yellow Pages. Their lives revolve around their Smartphones. They communicate by e-mail and text. Most of their e-mailing is done through social media platforms and the vast majority are done through Facebook. I have heard several major news stories from them which they have seen on Twitter or Facebook hours before those stories were on the traditional TV and radio news broadcasts. If you want to sell or communicate with this generation you need to spend some time and not much money to make sure you are not left behind. This phenomenon is not going away. In Ireland, over half of the population is under 35. Do you know what happens if someone searches for your company through Facebook?

To educate myself further I attended an interesting seminar on digital marketing given by an expert, a woman called Krishna De, who was formerly on the board of Diageo. When she was introduced at the start of the day she asked how many people tweeted. Four people put their hands up. She encouraged them to send a tweet during the morning and she gave out a Twitter domain for the venue.

When she started her session at 2pm she put up a live diagnostic screen which showed us that seven tweets had been sent from the room that morning. She could show us which tweets had been "re-tweeted" by the receivers, to their networks. By 2pm, over 39,000 people had received those seven tweets and the numbers were rising rapidly. Now that's pretty powerful communication. And it's free. If you don't understand all of this get expert help and decide on which parts of this you should be getting involved in.

To prepare a plan for your position on digital media you need to first think about what you want to achieve. Are you trying to heighten awareness of your brand, trying to improve your customer service by improving your online accessibility or trying to increase the number of visits/hits to your website? You should prioritise the audiences that you want to connect with – and then work out which media platforms they are using.

First establish your presence on one or two platforms only and get that right before going for more. You need to plan exactly what type of content you're going to put on your sites and the types of content you are going to send to your various audiences, be they your customers, suppliers, peer groups, forums or professional bodies. Will you be sending text, video and/or audio? There are endless opportunities to educate and engage with your customers, building your brand and markets at very low cost.

Make sure someone is properly trained to handle all of this – there are rules and regulations governing online content. Don't go breaking the law.

One large organisation I know, terrified about losing out to online competitors, gave smart phones to dozens of staff – and told them to "get tweeting". But they were given no training or guidelines and a barrage of inappropriate and damaging tweeting followed. Train your staff on "appropriateness" and "tone".

Lose your paranoia about your staff wasting their time all day online – if you set it up and monitor it properly you will get great value for money.

5. Your Online Image: Imagine someone wrote a derogatory newspaper article about you personally or your organisation. You would be fuming, ringing your solicitors and trying to limit the damage. Yet the longer you are in business, the more comment there is about you online – on social media sites and on forums etc, which is either boosting or damaging your reputation. Many organisations have no policy at all in relation to this but the issue is getting bigger.

Start by searching for yourself, your company and senior colleagues on Twitter, Facebook, Linked-In, YouTube, forums, boards etc and using different search engines. You'll probably be surprised at how much you find. Now search for key words relevant to your company. You need to think about the image of you that is developing online and what you can do about it. You should develop your own policy about how you respond to criticism and incorrect comment online and make sure your staff know what to do. If you are very "public facing" or if there is a particular problem online you could have a policy of responding in real time to maximise and protect your business. As a minimum you should establish what your current position is in relation to digital media and plan how you can take advantage of this new world.

There are some good, free online video tutorials for business on branding and social media etc e.g.:

www.Youtube.com/BizGrowthtv

www.facebook.com/BizgrowthMedia

An expert consultant is Krishna De-see KrishnaDe.com

// CHAPTER 17 //
DRESS TO IMPRESS

You only get one chance to make a first impression and the first impression you give of yourself is often the most important. In business people don't have the time or the energy to spare to allow you to try to convince them how good you are, if their first impression of you is that you don't look the part. You must look at least as good as your clients and customers expect you to look. If dress-sense does not come naturally to you this is another area where a little bit of thought and effort can have a big effect. Indeed, in business, if you are seen as being a good dresser, someone who always impresses with how they present themselves this alone enhances your image and your value. In the absence of any evidence to the contrary people will automatically assume that you perform at a high level in a whole range of skills because you look the business. If you dress poorly with badly fitting clothes, clashing colours, cheap or frayed clothes or with stains or marks, no matter how fantastic you are at your job, others will automatically downgrade your abilities. Harsh but true.

You must dress appropriately for the occasion. For men, in particular, there really is no excuse but it's amazing how many men get it so badly wrong. If in doubt, pick a dark suit, a good quality plain white or blue shirt (avoid checks) and a classic silk tie. The tie is one area where there is room to express a little flair and originality but if in doubt don't even try. Just keep it plain and simple. Choose good quality city shoes which you should polish every day. Your shoes should match the colour of your belt, i.e. don't mix black and brown. Knot your tie so that it reaches the top of your belt, no higher, no lower. Wear plain black socks. No funny colours, patterns or cartoon characters. Your hair should be neatly cut ideally every month. Don't leave it longer than six weeks. Now you are good to go.

My late grandfather Jim Connolly was a font of common sense and a great judge of people. He once said to me:"Paul, if you haven't got the time to spare to judge a man, have a look at his shoes. A man who couldn't be bothered polishing his shoes properly every day probably couldn't be bothered doing lots of things properly." He was right, of course, so keep that in mind. And as you are giving your shoes a good polish every morning, remind yourself about the extra little effort, the extra "polish" you are going to add to your performance that day, and how that little extra effort is going to make you outstanding.

Dressing for Women: All of the same principles apply in that you must dress appropriately and at least as well as is expected of you. For women, there is far more room for variety but unfortunately far more room for disaster as well. Badly-dressed women in business is the one issue guaranteed to turn the best managers into nervous wrecks. It is difficult to tell a woman, whether a peer or an employee, that they are dressing badly or inappropriately. From experience, most managers (especially male) fail to deal with the problem and hope that it will go away. It won't. It will get worse. Indeed, if other work colleagues see someone "getting away" with dressing sloppily over time, they are quite likely to start dropping their own standards leading to damage to your business. Staff uniforms are one possible answer but there are often problems in enforcing adherence to the uniform guidelines as over time staff may take shortcuts or experiment with the rules. If a uniform code isn't strictly enforced you'll end up with a bigger mess. I certainly won't attempt to give guidance on women's dress but there are lots of professional stylists available who will help you choose your wardrobe and will accompany you on shopping trips. Be professional about your appearance.

The famous model Grace O'Shaughnessy was engaged by the estate agency in the 1990s to advise all of the staff on styling. She told me that I had "the American Senatorial look". She didn't say whether I was Republican or Democrat but I guess I know what she meant. For men and women if in doubt over-dress not under-dress. Take care and pride in your appearance. You are representing yourself, your colleagues and your organisation and that's a responsibility you should take seriously.

There is a trend worldwide not to wear a tie particularly in cities in hotter climates and this is often entirely appropriate. In certain industries, e.g. IT and architecture, it is quite normal not to wear a tie. If you are meeting anyone in a business context, for example, pitching for work, and all of your potential clients are not wearing ties, and all of your Team are, that is not going to ease a connection between the groups. However, the opposite case is worse where you find yourself in a situation not wearing a tie but your clients/potential clients are. That can make you look casual and ill-prepared. So err on the side of slightly "over-dressing".

Recently, I made a video, which is on my website paulmcneive.com. I prepared well and decided to wear a suit, shirt and no tie. The day was cold and got windy so I wore a coat. I was happy with the result but I knew I should take advice from a couple of experts in the "image business". Conrad Jones watched it with me and commented as it went along. "Yeah, nice suit, great backdrop, hair is blowing around too much, nice bit of passion, coat looks a bit crumpled, you look a bit pale. And you should have worn a tie. I know it's trendy and all that, but at the end of the day, the guys signing the big cheques are all wearing ties."

I was a bit taken aback but he was absolutely right.

A week later I remade the video, same setting with the same script. This time I'd had my hair cut, my coat dry-cleaned and I was wearing a tie. Also I had hired a stylist who sprayed my hair (so it didn't matter when the wind blew) and also applied make-up as any TV presenter would always wear. The remake cost very little more to do but looks 30 per cent more professional. Never be shy to look for advice when you are stepping into an area where you are not an expert. And never accept second best, either from yourself or anyone else. Make sure that everything that you do is your absolute best possible effort.

When dressing for business, keep that "appropriate" word in mind. It may be entirely appropriate on occasions to dress differently from your clients, for example, in the more creative sectors. Take the case of a company which has just decided to invest heavily in a major marketing campaign and they've invited in a marketing/advertising consultancy to pitch for the business. If those marketing people troop in all dressed very conservatively the clients may well be disappointed. They are looking for a spark, for creativity and that's why in the advertising business, you'll see designer gear, lots of black polo necks and long sideburns etc.

Similarly in architecture, some of the guys at the very top of the creative tree, known as "Starchitects", dress like rock stars and it works.

Daniel Libeskind dresses like Bono and wears the most amazing cowboy boots with the longest curling pointed toes I've ever seen. Is it appropriate? Yes. Don't forget, you are looking to make it easy for those clients to remember you and flamboyant edgy dress is almost required of a leading architect. However, let's say that that architect designs a stunning skyscraper – do you want the structural engineer who is calculating how to make the building stay up also dressing like a rock star with pointy boots? Probably not. His professional role is more conservative and his dress should reflect that. So, allied professions, on the same job, but different standards of "appropriateness".

I've noticed that a lot of architects, engineers and surveyors dress in check jackets, lots of greens and browns etc – all a bit "earthy". It's appropriate – the clients may expect you to be a little bit different or creative but there is a huge danger of pigeon-holing yourself at a certain level or role which can work against you. You may not be seen as a top business person, dynamic and strategic, someone who adds real extra value to the team even outside your brief. The most successful architects, engineers and quantity surveyors I know, dress like top businessmen, ready for the Boardroom. You should too.

Again for certain sectors and occasions, dressing "quirky" can be entirely appropriate. One of the best motivational speakers I have seen is Watt Nicoll. He is in his seventies, a big man with lots of white hair and a beard. He wears a suit, but always with bright red braces and a dramatic novelty bowtie. He often changes his bowtie several times a day. This works because you expect something different from a motivational speaker. The bowties have become part of Watt's image. You'll always remember him. So, "different" can be good, but getting much closer to "quirky" is dangerous; it could worry some clients and could lose you work.

I have never liked the modern trend of "dress-down Friday" where everyone wears "smart casual" clothes rather than their normal professional outfit. The big problem is that it is hard enough to keep everyone looking smart and professional in the context of formal business attire but when people are allowed to wear their own interpretation of "smart casual", the results are often disastrous. I have been in many companies on "dress-down Fridays" where the scene looked more like a refugee camp than a professional operation.

Never let someone in your business continue to dress inappropriately. You must confront the issue but be sure of your ground and you may need to take advice. Be especially careful where dealing with the opposite sex. What one person thinks looks stylish and professional another may regard as a complete mess. If you are a male challenging the appearance of a female you should ensure that you have at least one other woman at management level involved in the meeting. This provides better balance and I have also seen dress code issues complicated by pregnancy and menstruation.

For all ages and all sexes, dress code, grooming and styling is hugely important. It's also often emotional. You must manage it but take all the expert advice that you can get.

Challenge yourself to always look the best that you can. A wise piece of advice from my sister Sheila, a stylist: "Dress for the job that you want, not the job that you have."

Being Photographed: I think we are all uncomfortable having our photograph taken – I certainly am. Do try to smile with your eyes as well as your mouth. The best tip I ever got from a photographer was to lean forward slightly towards the camera. Try it – it makes a big difference. Don't let a photographer tell you to fold your arms; you will look uneasy and aggressive. Feel free to shoot the next photographer who tells a group of you to stare dreamily at some point in the clouds. You will look ridiculous.

// CHAPTER 18 //
QUALITY STANDARDS

Hmmmm. Quality Standard Accreditation is very common now in most business areas and I came across another version in the last few years as the National Rehabilitation Hospital successfully gained accreditation to the international C.A.R.F. healthcare standard. In some business areas you can't be awarded a job unless you have a certain accreditation.

I can speak with some authority on this because in the nineties I was struck by the novel idea of gaining the Quality Mark for an estate agents services. We successfully achieved that and the company then went on to achieve ISO 9000 accreditation for quality of service. Apart from the fact that you may need accreditation to secure government work, here are some pros and cons:

1. Quality Standards grew out of manufacturing industry particularly pharmaceuticals and armaments where the consistency and quality of the products had to be extremely high. The problems and defects were easily enough identified – cracks, wrong size, wrong shape, wrong ingredients etc. But when interest developed in bringing quality standards into the services industries, problems arose because it was much more difficult to measure customer satisfaction with service and various human inputs. A good effort was made but the quality standards for manufacturing were bent to try to fit the service industry – thus producing some very clumsy language. For example in quality standard language, a "mistake" is a "non-conformance" which doesn't help when you're trying to teach and enthuse an audience. However, as I gained experience and confidence I had great fun rewriting the company's quality manuals into plain English.

2. Personally I've never come across a service company that works its quality system fully as part of the daily routine as it's supposed to be. Often, you'll find quality manuals and procedures manuals gathering dust at the back of bookshelves or buried somewhere on the company IT system. More positively it is at least a central place for writing everything down. For example, the quality manual contains the company's objectives and mission statement and a family tree organisational structure which is useful. Procedures manuals, where the task is clearly written and explained, can be a helpful reminder – especially to junior staff on what to do next and you can write in "red flags", that is points at which a junior cannot proceed without seeking assistance. Having everything written down in one place is very useful at the induction stage for new staff.

3. A functioning quality system does allow you monitor and measure whether your quality of service is improving or disimproving. (Many organisations think they're providing a good service mostly because "we don't get many complaints") A big problem is clients getting tired of responding to questionnaires and your information dries up. I found the 'mystery shopping' format easier for getting information and there's no reason why that can't be incorporated into a company's quality system.

4. Complaints: You must have a complaints procedure and staff must be trained to follow it. Overall I believe this improves how a company deals with complaints. The proper recording and dating of information and complaints will always stand to you. I saw a dispute between a company and a client end up in court. There were stark differences of opinion over what had happened, who said what and when. On the face of it, it was hard to say who was correct but the staff member had a very orderly file and could demonstrate that he had correctly followed the company's complaints procedures. The judge was impressed by the orderliness and accuracy of the file notes,as they added weight to the company's case and found in favour of the company. (As an aside, develop a habit of making a brief note of important business conversations especially negotiations. Date your note, initial it, add the time of the conversation, and put in inverted commas the exact relevant quotations. This practice will stand you in good stead time and time again if disputes arise.) I also recommend that you routinely download and keep your text messages and keep your old SIM card when you change phones. I once saw a business dispute over who had said what decisively settled when one party produced a text message off a sim card they had kept for several years. Game, set and match. When disputes arise you will always be best positioned if you have accurate records as the other side probably won't.

5. Quality systems can pick up things you may not think of: A company I worked with saved a lot of money when an internal audit drew attention to the amount of actions that had to be taken and paperwork created when someone generated a credit note, i.e. cancelling or replacing an earlier invoice. It turned out that eleven different things then had to happen; the salesperson dictated a credit note, a secretary typed it, a copy went on the file, a blue copy went to accounts, a pink copy to someone else in accounts, a copy went to the client with a new invoice and statement. Accounts then had to input the change into their system etc, etc, etc. The audit also showed that the company had issued 124 credit notes in the previous 12 months – so the cost of all that time wasted was significant. But the biggest cost was that the invoice would be delayed further before being paid; at least another month which was affecting cashflow. A detailed look at why the company issued so many credit notes demonstrated that whilst some were to correct errors in the original invoice, the majority were because the client had asked for the invoice to be readdressed to a different party. For example, instead of the client being invoiced personally he wanted it invoiced to a company or vice versa. More typically an invoice would be issued to a company and the client would then ask for the invoice to be made out to a different company in his group. We made sure that everyone now telephoned their client before issuing an invoice to double-check to whom it should be invoiced. Instantly the number of credit notes more than halved and cashflow improved. I've since discovered that this is a problem in lots of companies so check how many credit notes you are issuing and why.

With so many companies going into examinership, receivership or liquidation or where you are supplying receivers who are running businesses, it's vital that your contract is with the correct legal entity or you may not be entitled to be paid. You should also check-up on your largest, longest standing customers. Are you still being paid by the company or entity with which you think you have a contract? Frequently, something has changed and you may find that you are exposed.

6. Quality systems can give you a competitive edge but approach with caution. If you're considering implementing one you must keep it simple.

Everything you say you're going to do you must audit, i.e. prove that you did it. If you're considering engaging a consultant to help you implement a system for you, ask to visit one of his clients, talk to them and read their manuals. If their client doesn't really understand the whole thing, if the manuals are complicated and the staff think so too then find another consultant.

Quality systems can be a good way of bringing people together on a drive for quality but if you don't keep it very simple and user friendly your staff will move from a position of enthusiasm to apathy and even to resentment of all this paperwork getting in the way of their work. And that's not good.

Handle with care.

// CHAPTER 19 //
REACH FOR THE SKY

As a child I was fascinated by aeroplanes. I built dozens of airfix models which hung on threads from the ceiling of my bedroom. I devoured the Biggles Books. Over my bed was a massive poster of aeroplanes on the apron at Dublin Airport courtesy of my Grandfather Jim who worked in the control tower. I dreamed of being a pilot. For some reason on leaving school I never pursued a career as a pilot. I wasn't great at maths and it seemed just impossible to be one of the tiny numbers being taken on as trainees by the airlines. I never even tried.

In the mid-90s my late uncle, Brian Connolly, who had been a squadron leader in the RAF, was President of the Dublin Gliding Club, operating from Punchestown. I decided to try my hand at gliding. Brian taught me the basics of gliding in an old, timber, two-man training glider. (Folks, believe me, you haven't lived until you find yourself in an old timber glider with no power, being pulled steeply upwards through the clouds, on the end of a chain by a small plane.) I continued gliding and Brian also gave me some lessons flying the 'tug' as the plane pulling up the glider is known. But in smaller aircraft I was seated or lying almost prone or cramped and I had little control over the right pedal. I could only operate the right pedal by pushing down on my prosthetic knee with my right elbow whilst still holding the joystick – a manoeuvre unlikely to see me licenced anywhere.

Someone suggested that I try helicopters as the pilot sits more upright. I telephoned a flying school at Weston Airport. I told them my situation and asked if I could come and sit in one of their helicopters. After only a slight hesitation the Chief Pilot, Paul Noctor, agreed. Once I sat into the helicopter I found I had great pedal control as the pedals are counter-balanced and I could operate them properly using my prosthetic legs. Paul kindly offered to bring me for a short flight and I was smitten. What an incredible sensation. I decided that I would become a helicopter pilot.

Learning to fly helicopters was exhilarating, frustrating, challenging and hugely rewarding. It reminded me of the process of "Small Steps" that make up a programme of rehabilitation. There's many a day when you come in from the airfield feeling that you have made little progress and there are other days where you seem to make great strides. But no step can be left out and you have to keep going relentlessly if you want to succeed.

The hardest part of learning to fly a helicopter is actually 'the hover', that is keeping the aircraft hovering in one spot, particularly if it's windy. Doing this you have to operate four different sensitive controls with your feet and both hands simultaneously. Any input to one control effects all the others. It's a balancing act. The training pilot can only tell you so much – after that you just have to find the 'sweet spot' yourself. This can be highly frustrating; you sometimes think you'll never get there. It often takes trainees around 10 hours of practicing before suddenly one day – Wow. Something clicks and you're suddenly hovering on your own. It's a bit like that feeling you got when you first successfully rode a bike.

Getting my licence became a priority for me and I allocated Sunday afternoons to attend groundschool where you prepare for your exams on air law, meteorology and navigation etc. There was plenty of study required too but that wasn't too difficult as I couldn't wait to learn more.

I practised and practised my flying and was approaching being "signed-out" as competent for my first solo flight. For that I needed a student licence. To get one I needed to pass a pilot's medical and that's where progress slowed up. I was aware that there were commercial jet pilots licensed with one prosthetic leg or wearing glasses but the "system" just couldn't cope with the notion of a helicopter pilot with no legs! The lesson here, and one I learned many times throughout life is to stay calm and reasonable rather than to get stroppy with the authorities and try to force them into doing something which rarely works. (I had also noticed at the National Rehabilitation Hospital that the patients who had the best outcomes were those who submitted to the system – including the parts they didn't like. Those who complained, argued and didn't turn up for therapy never did as well). I have also learnt that it is better and easier to effect change by working with people and bringing them with you to where you want to go – rather than trying to force them from a distance. Play the system.

I stayed calm, although my first solo flight was delayed for months. Eventually someone pointed out to me that there was an Englishman, a Dr. Tallent, working in the Aeromedical Examination unit at the Mater Hospital who had experience of prosthetics. I went to see him and he was extremely helpful in promoting my case with the aviation authority. The impasse was eventually broken when my instructor suggested to them that they should send an inspector to assess my flying on a student basis in a helicopter with dual controls. They agreed and sent two senior inspectors to the flying school at Weston Airport. Naturally I was very nervous as we were all introduced outside the flying school's portacabin office. One of the inspectors asked me if I had much power in my prosthetic legs. There was a plank leaning against the portacabin and instinctively I took a couple of steps over and with my below-knee prosthesis, I kicked it a few yards away. "Fair enough," said the Inspector with a grin. Kicking planks is not a medical test set out in any aviation manuals but it was a good start.

We went out to a four seater Robinson 44 Helicopter with dual-controls; I in the flying seat, my instructor next to me and the two Inspectors in the back seats. The plan was to do a few manoeuvres which would particularly test my pedal control and then some circuits. They had suggested a 45 minute flight. Heart pounding and with my brow covered in perspiration I lifted us up into a hover and held it before performing two 360° degree rotations in each direction, stopping every 90°. With my instructor making a big show of not touching the controls we then took off over the Liffey. I was just halfway around a circuit of the airport when I heard a voice in my headphones from one of the inspectors behind:

"Thanks very much gentlemen. Sorry for wasting your time. You can take us back in whenever you like."

My student licence was issued a few days later and that week I had the incredible, heart-thumping experience of soaring out over the Liffey flying a helicopter on my own. I continued my training, to include mastering "autorotations" which is the manoeuvre you perform if you have a power failure in flight. When this happens, either because of an engine failure or gearbox/powertrain failure, the speed of your rotors quickly decreases. Instantly an alarm sounds as the rotors reduce to about 85 per cent of normal speed and you have only a second or two to react or you will crash. The reaction is to rapidly but smoothly lower the collective, (like putting in the clutch), and which also reduces the angle of attack of your rotor blades and preserves their speed. You lower the right pedal (to stop the helicopter spinning), and put the nose up to increase airflow through your rotors. You establish the helicopter in a stable attitude and you must keep the rotor speed in the required range. You turn into the wind (to slow you up and increase airflow through your rotors), make your emergency radio call and now look for the best available landing site, all the time watching out for wires and livestock. (Properly set up, even a small Robinson 22 two seater, with a power failure at 1000 feet, can glide for a mile).

You glide towards your landing site and at about 40 feet off the ground you "flare" the aircraft, that is to fairly steeply raise the nose upwards. This is to slow you down and give you a last valuable boost of airflow through those freewheeling rotors. Then you level the helicopter and do a run-on landing using the collective and that last bit of energy in the rotors to cushion your landing. It's one of the most necessary, exhilarating and difficult manoeuvres in flying helicopters. That's partly because the stakes are so high; you only get one shot at it. The critical point is to react quickly to the power failure when you're up in the sky. If you delay and allow the rotor speed to reduce too far you can't get it back and the helicopter will drop uncontrollably.

Once you preserve your rotor speed the craft remains controllable and the aim is to get it into a level glide low over the ground. Even if you make a botch of the touchdown, at least you're now probably looking at a survivable accident. The autorotation, quite properly, has to be successfully performed to pass your test and again at every annual safety test.

One overcast day in 2000, having passed the academic exams, I took my test for my full private pilot's licence. Not by fluke, perhaps, I had been assigned "The Grim Reaper" of examiners renowned for his high failure rate. After a technical grilling with models of helicopters and a forensic examination of my knowledge of the various parts of the aircraft at the machine, we set off. The test involves a tough series of manoeuvres including 360° turns, figures of eight, reversing, emergency stops, power failures while hovering, landings and take-offs in congested areas and also of your radio proficiency. Then you're off to do a few circuits of the airfield followed by a navigational test (no GPS allowed) to some remote airfield. Miss it first time and you fail your test. On the way back, usually, comes the emergency power failure. The examiner gives you a short warning.

"Emergency power failure in three seconds. Three, two, one," then he closes the throttle on his side disconnecting your power. All the hours and hours of training took over as I calmly worked through the procedures and managed a nice smooth run-on landing in a field somewhere near Maynooth. Then it was up again and back to Weston. More detailed questioning as I shut down the aircraft; no change of expression as he led me back to the office and began questioning me again on some point I had hesitated on in the morning grilling. Completely drenched in sweat and my brain beginning to shut down at this stage, he sat back in his chair and gave a little smile.

"Congratulations Paul. Your flying's very good. I'm passing you."

Wow, what an adrenaline rush and a great feeling of accomplishment. I floated on air for days and I soon received my full licence. I was now licenced to fly two and four seater aircraft anywhere in the world. As my instructor said: "You can't buy that."

Months later I noticed that a magazine was available from a British disabled pilots club. I subscribed and filled in the form detailing my disability and the type of aircraft I flew. A few days later the phone rang and it was the secretary of that club.

"Paul, we got your application, thanks for that. We were a bit taken aback here when we saw you're flying helicopters. I've looked into it a bit and as far as we can ascertain, you're the first double amputee to get a helicopter pilots licence in the world."

First in the world; now that can't be bad.

Everything I learnt through this achievement, underlies what I've learnt in all areas of life:

1. Reach for the sky – Don't be afraid to dream. The little boy who dreamed of one day being a pilot eventually lived that dream even though he had no legs.

2. Everything is possible: With your dream, hard work and tenacity you can achieve anything you want no matter how improbable it may initially appear. Just because no one else has ever achieved something before doesn't mean that you have not got the power and ability to achieve it. You do.

3. Don't let others talk you down: Never let anyone try and discourage you from achieving your dreams. It was probably a good thing that no one knew at the outset (including me) that what I was attempting had never been done before. That might have stopped me trying.

4. Achieving that goal took work, focus and a plan: I had to be focused and unstoppable to achieve my goal. My plan of "Kneebends" or "Small Steps" was essentially the syllabus for the flying exam and the academic exams – all the individual items that had to be conquered. The timetable of groundschool classes over months was another step in the plan. I never gave up. I persevered until I found a way around every single obstacle, especially the medical licencing issues.

5. DREAM + PLAN + WORK = SUCCESS: It's easy to stay motivated and to do the work when you love what you're doing. Can you find a job that you love? If you can, you'll never feel like you're working again.

A few interesting related points:

(a) Weston Airport, Co. Kildare, which was the base for my training and my test was used before its refurbishment as the set for RAF bases in several films, notably The Blue Max. The airfield was visited by the legendary Douglas Bader, the famous legless pilot from World War II. Apart from being an ace pilot and squadron leader, Bader, who had lost his legs in a flying accident is recognised as being pivotal in the allied forces winning the war. At a late stage in the war RAF fighter command eventually accepted his strategic advice on tactical flying formations and began massing squadrons together which proved successful.

(b) I've also learned that I have the exact same injuries as Bader, that is a below the knee amputation on the left and above the knee on the right. I was struck by similarities in his own experiences of the whole limb-fitting procedure to mine, in his autobiography "Reach for the Sky".

(c) My pilot's licence gained some humorous notoriety in the aeronautical medical field. One year while completing my pilots medical examination the doctor blinked and looked puzzled as he inserted an updated certificate into my licence. "I don't believe it," he said, "Can I take a copy of this?" I said "Sure, why?" He began laughing again and pointed at the "conditions/endorsements" section where strict specific medical provisions are endorsed on the licence, e.g. "Licence holder must wear prescribed corrective lenses and must carry an accessible spare pair of glasses when flying." My licence was completely blank. The most disabled helicopter pilot in the world had no medical endorsements whatsoever on his licence. A funny little anomaly and a classic case of a system struggling to cope with something which didn't fit. For my subsequent licences they adopted my suggestion of "Licence Holder must wear artificial limbs"!

(d) I once visited Biggin Hill aerodrome in England. I was chatting with a friend when I noticed a man in a wheelchair emerging from an office. He wheeled himself out to the side of a small plane and using his arms hauled himself into the cockpit pulling a strap behind him. He pulled in the strap and his wheelchair rose up the side of the aircraft. He grabbed it, folded it and pulled it into the plane. Then he flew away. Written in blue letters on the nose of the aircraft were the words, "Advance with calm". What a powerful message for life which I have always remembered and tried to adopt. "Advance with calm."

(e) I had an emotional experience connected with flying. One day when flying on my own I couldn't resist the temptation to go and fly over Dr. Steevens Hospital where I had spent all those months in the Burns Unit. Carefully observing the flying restrictions over the Phoenix Park, I followed the railway lines to Heuston Station and suddenly, right below me, there was the hospital. I did a few circuits of the buildings and I could even see the window into my old room. Bizarrely I noticed some large yellow metal incinerators in the back yard and I wondered if my legs had been incinerated in there after they were amputated. But most of all I got a lovely warm feeling. I felt happy. It wasn't all that long since those three doctors told me they would have to amputate my legs. None of us could have imagined that I would soon be flying overhead. It felt good.

// CHAPTER 20 //
MOTIVATION - GET YOUR MOJO WORKING!

In business, most people are motivated by their need to earn a living; to provide for their family –which is a strong driver. You're lucky if you are also motivated by the love of your job and your desire to be the very best that you can because success will follow and your job will appear to be easy to you. You must always be aware of the power of your attitude and actions to either motivate or de-motivate those around you particularly if you are a leader. Your colleagues will be drawn to and motivated by your enthusiastic "can-do" attitude to all of your work. As a leader the most de-motivating thing you can do is to allow a vacuum to develop where your staff get no feedback on how they are doing, no praise and no enthusiasm for their suggestions. This vacuum will kill creativity and extra effort. Publicly recognise, praise and reward the extra efforts and successes of your staff. They will then try even harder. Discreetly, honestly and fairly, point out to individuals where they are not performing to standard and offer advice. Do not let performance issues fester.

As a leader your staff will look to you for direction and motivation. Your own behaviour all day, every day, must be the best example you can give. From time to time events and opportunities will occur where your business will benefit from an injection of motivation. Treat those occasions seriously.

A few years ago I was asked in to do some training for a sales and distribution company. Business was good and they were the largest and most profitable company in their sector. Everyone was working flat out and earning good money. The owner asked me to participate in their annual training and team building day, and to speak about customer service and motivation. During the briefing he mentioned that earlier in the year they had lost a contract to a smaller competitor. It was their oldest customer and the change had caused some waves in his business. Some of his competitors had seen it as an opportunity to headhunt some of his key staff by offering attractive packages to move. He was upset to hear back that his competitors were saying at these interviews that his company was "past it". Some of his staff had received e-mails from people in other rival firms mocking them over the loss of this customer. The owner was trying to keep a lid on things.

I suggested that an option for him was to consider something very different. He listened to my suggestion and agreed.

On the day I broke the sales people into different teams, and we talked about service, their competitors and targets for the next year. Spirits were high. The time came for the owner's closing remarks. He praised his staff and told them that the company was at an important stage, challenged with replacing the business they had lost with their biggest customer. He especially thanked the staff for their loyalty. Then he invited a star salesman to speak. This young man stood up and related to his colleagues what their competitor had said about them being "past it" when they tried to recruit him. A young woman told of a similar experience – their competitor had laughed at them and said they were a spent force. A third man then told a similar story. You could have heard a pin drop in the room. Then the boss asked three other members of staff to read out mocking e-mails they had received from competitors. There was a shocked silence in the room but you could almost hear the blood boiling. The owner chose his moment and said: "I hope you guys will join me in spending the next year shoving these insults down their throats."

Loud cheers! One of the salesmen jumped up, walked to the top of the room where their competitors logos were on a display stand and kicked them across the room. He was quickly joined by several others in kicking the logos into smithereens, to even louder cheers. I was delighted.

That company increased its sales turnover by more than a third the following year. I had used the old football manager's motivational tactics of "they're all against us". It works because when you find an opportunity to inject passion, emotion and motivation into your organisation at critical stages there will almost always be a positive response.

I'm hoping that some of my stories and ideas have at least made you pause and think about how your run your operation. Hopefully you will be inspired to make a fresh start with a new approach and energy.

You have the ability to achieve anything you can imagine: But why do most of us settle for much less than our potential – for being ordinary? I think the answer is that most of us lack the motivation to effect real change in our lives. We settle for what we have and hope that things will change for the better. We feel that things aren't going too badly; we're in a routine, we're in a groove. But another name for a groove is a 'rut'. And nothing's going to change unless you set out to change it.

I think it's a human condition to revert to what is ordinary and normal for us. Every now and then I find myself at a funeral of someone young who has died from an illness or accident. Sometimes there's a couple of funerals close together and they often have a big impact on me. These events shock you into stopping and thinking about life and many times I resolved to change something in my life. Yet, days later, I'm usually straight back rushing around in the same old ways.

I suggest that it's time to stop hoping that things are going to pick up. It's time to stop thinking that it is only a few people who can achieve extraordinary things. We all can. You can too. You're special. Allow yourself to dream and visualise what it will feel like when you have achieved your goal.

With a little cajoling most of us can temporarily come up with a dream or something we'd like to achieve. But we often don't even start the work to achieve that goal because we're so conditioned by a fear of failure. We are surrounded by opportunities. Be inspired by those amazing sports stars and business people who seem to achieve success at everything. They started out as 'ordinary' just like the rest of us. But they were prepared to put in the work to achieve their goal and they let nothing stop them. That's not magic. We can all do that.

*   *   *   *

I have always found that visualising yourself in a good situation in the future, a technique first taught to me in hospital, works very well for me and I urge you to try it. The top golfers in the world visualise every shot before they hit it. If you do that, then when you take action you're more likely to get the right result. Emphasising the importance of positive thinking there's a great quotation by Henry Ford: "Whether you think you'll fail or succeed – you're probably right."

If things are going badly for you, if you're on a bad run, a good thing to do is to remember and think through exactly what you were doing the last time you had a great success. Remember how you felt after winning that new business. You need to renew that positive energy in yourself to get back on the winning track.

Early in my career I was sent to Dundalk to try to win instructions to sell a large factory there. I had my hair cut, wore my very best suit, shirt and tie and washed the car. That meeting went very well and I won those instructions on my own. I remember driving back from Dundalk. The sun was shining. The car was shining. I was shining. I turned up the volume on Lizzy's "The Boys Are Back in Town" and hit the gas. I felt great. I was a winner. And nice mileage expenses for the journey too.

Many times during my career I would wash the car, wear my best suit and play that song on the drive to a meeting. It instantly brought back that winning feeling. Why don't you try recreating your best moments – because it works.

A little guiltily, another thing I do when times are tough is to think about people I know who are suffering from bad health to realise how lucky I am and to get my act together. My problems are tiny by comparison. Doing that doesn't always feel quite right, but it stops me feeling sorry for myself. And it works.

Motivation is that mental bridge between a thought and action. Some people don't even seem to have to think about this; they bounce out of bed early, full of vigour and take on the world. Most of us are not naturally like that and the answer for us is to draw up your plan of action to achieve your goal. Your plan is your bridge to get you from your thoughts into taking consistent action and achieving your goals. I spent a lot of time in Chapter One emphasising the importance of your plan of "Small Steps," those little 'kneebends' that when added together will amount to something huge for you.

The biggest single change you can make in your life is to write down your goals and how you are going to achieve them. You are now taking control of your life. Stop getting pushed around. Write down your goals for your personal and your business life. Then write down your timetable for achieving them.

Now, you're changing things.

As you begin to achieve new successes you will experience a warm glow of accomplishment, a pride in yourself; that lovely feeling when you win a new job, gain promotion, earn your pilot's license or learn to play an instrument. This is largely caused by your body releasing dopamine into your brain – that's a neurotransmitter responsible for feelings of pleasure. It feels great and you'll want more of it. So don't settle for ordinary or second best – go for it.

A WINNING MINDSET

Try your hardest to maintain a positive can-do attitude in everything you do. Never underestimate the power of a winning mindset on both you and those around you as it can bring you and your company to an even higher level of success. A few years ago I noticed a photograph in the newspaper of a smiling Tiger Woods putting a winner's blazer on Padraig Harrington. The caption told me that Harrington had beaten Woods in a play-off to win the Dunlop Invitational Tournament in Ohio. The next line of text blew me away. "This is the first time that Tiger Woods has been beaten in a play-off in the U.S."

I checked Tiger Woods' record further. It turns out that Tiger Woods had then played eleven play-offs on the PGA Tour and lost just one. On the European Tour he had played in 10 play-offs and had won every one. This is astounding.

By definition the golfers in the play-off are playing the same quality of golf. They're inseparable after four days of playing. If there was any logic to this process Tiger Woods would win about half of his play-offs (or less, as sometimes there are three or four golfers in the play-off.) But Tiger Woods' record up to this year was: Played 25 play-offs. Won 23. Lost 2.

There is obviously a major extra force coming into play here. The answer is simply that Tiger *knows* he is going to win the play-off. That is the strength of his positive attitude. Every play-off he won made it even more certain that he would win the next. Success breeds success.

Crucially his play-off opponents despite being full of confidence and playing at the top of their game also know that Tiger is going to win. Woods' caddie (his staff) knows that Tiger's going to win. His opponent's caddie (the competition's staff) also knows that Tiger's going to win and that his man is going to come up short. Everyone in the crowd at the golf course knows the same thing. Ditto all those watching on television. There is only one outcome – Tiger will defy all scientific logic and win. 23 wins. Two losses.

That's the power of a winning mindset and how powerfully it can affect you, your staff, your competitors and your market. Tiger subsequently lost his way in life and his record in play-offs hasn't been tested for some time. I wouldn't bet against his return to the top of the game but the example of his mental invincibility over those years holds true.

Many years ago I realised that when times were tough in business, when I was having a bad run and needed something to get things going again, the answer is always to get out into your marketplace and meet as many people as possible. You have to shake yourself out of that rut and that losing mindset. A while back, U2 were playing concerts in Dublin and I had assumed (wrongly) that it would be easy to get good gigs for my Bono act. I had a couple arranged but not enough and I wanted to have some gigs in the city centre. Armed with stacks of my flyers I called into virtually every large pub from Grafton Street to Temple Bar. They were all busy and I had left it too late. I didn't get one new gig even though I spent most of the day at it and must have visited 20 venues. I was tired, sore and despondent. Just before getting on the Luas back home I gave it one more shot – I wasn't going to go home with absolutely nothing. I asked for the manager in Synnots which is a big pub on St. Stephen's Green. I showed him my brochure and told him I would appear and sing as Bono for €50.

He agreed.

The next evening I did the gig. The pub was busy and it went well with lots of people looking for photographs. Afterwards an American woman came up to me and said how much she had enjoyed it. She was with a high-end US travel agency that takes clients on city tours,centred on rock music concerts. Her group were staying in the Fitzwilliam Hotel next door. She asked if I would perform my act at their dinner the next night, before the concert. I agreed and that fee more than paid for a month of knocking on doors. And I have always found that that's what works to get yourself out of a rut. Get out there and meet people. Even if you have to take on some work at a very poor fee, it's better than playing with Facebook and you'll invariably meet someone which leads to a better opportunity. When times are tough keep going and always knock on one more door.

Here's a little device I sometimes use to keep pressure on myself to actually do the work towards achieving a goal. Tell some friends about the goal you are going to achieve. You won't want them to see you failing or as "all talk and no action". Even better, tell some people you don't like!

One of the most effective ways I have of motivating myself, when I'm faced with a few options on what to do next, is simply to ask myself: "What would a Canary do now?" Because, like all of us, I'd like to think of myself as operating at Canary levels as much as possible, this usually forces me to choose the right option – even though that sometimes involves more effort. So the next time you have a choice of paths to take, ask yourself: "Am I going to act like a Canary, a Robin or a Dodo?"

In 1957 Muddy Waters sang about "Got my Mojo Workin'". Your mojo is your self-belief, your ability to bounce back from setbacks and to overcome any negativity around you. Your mojo is your positive attitude, your charm and your power of attraction. When you start combining your goal-setting with taking that little extra time to be outstanding with your clients, then you will have your mojo working for you too...

CHAPTER 21

DOES HE TAKE SUGAR?

Many years before my accident I watched a documentary called "Does he take sugar?" It was about the phenomenon experienced by wheelchair users whereby people assume that you are less intelligent, completely stupid or something to be pitied and patronised just because you are in a wheelchair. In other words, when serving a wheelchair user a cup of tea people are inclined to ask somebody with you: "Does he take sugar?" instead of asking you. As if you wouldn't know yourself or couldn't handle the question.

Unfortunately I have to tell you that this phenomenon is a reality and if all this book does is reverse that perception by one per cent then it's worthwhile. It's a horrible and demeaning thing to have happen to you when you are in a wheelchair.

I still laugh when I remember my first experience of this. It occurred during my first few weeks in "the Rehab". My mother was spending long hours there and as always she was becoming great friends with all of the people she met in the visitors' canteen. One day she told me all about this lovely woman she had met whose daughter had injured her back and was on another ward. She asked me to come and meet them and I said I'd come up when I had finished some class or other. A little while later I wheeled myself up to the ward and I spotted my mother sitting on the end of a bed talking ninety to the dozen with another woman. I wheeled over and stopped a discreet distance from the end of the bed. The girl in the bed caught my eye and smiled and I waited politely for a pause in the two mothers' conversation. This was taking a while so while I was waiting I assumed one of my favourite expressions, a polite half-smile, with my eyebrows slightly raised, suggestive of great intelligence and strength yet sensitivity and emotional depth. Eventually, the other woman looked at me so I broadened my smile.

"Aw," said the woman turning to my mother, "Does he have a brain injury as well?"

It's hard to believe but this is the type of thing that people say when confronted with a wheelchair. I experienced a few examples of people ignoring me or talking over my head and in those first few years I realised that I was going to have to "toughen up" a bit and stand up for myself in some situations. A good example of this was my car insurance. When I got back driving, my insurance premium now included a 20 per cent "disabled driver's loading" from a large insurance company. I paid this loading for many years without thinking about it. I was just glad to be back on the road.

One evening I met an acquaintance who was a senior claims inspector with that company. We were talking about the cost of insurance and I casually mentioned the 20 per cent disabled driver's loading. He was taken aback and told me, firmly off the record, that his company knew well that the incidence of claims from disabled drivers was below the average. I should have been getting a reduction. They may as well have been loading my premium because I had brown eyes. They were conning me. The next day I rang that insurance company and queried my "disabled drivers" loading. On what basis were they loading me? A member of staff stonewalled me with clichés about risk assessment and company policy. I know she was looking at my description as "double amputee" and believe me when I say I recognised the patient and patronising tone of voice. She really thought that she was dealing with someone who "wasn't all there".

I called again the next day and got a similar response from another staff member. Now I knew what I had to do. Wearing my very best business suit I drove to the head office, approached the public desk and repeated my query as to why they were loading me. But now I'm standing there in front of them and I don't fit the image they have of the disabled driver on the phone. They were thrown by this and I got different treatment. They still couldn't answer my question but we were now discussing the matter as equals. I asked then to speak to a manager who came out to see me. He foolishly suggested my policy was loaded because there would be a longer delay in my reaction time before braking in an emergency. I politely pointed out that my hand was permanently on the accelerator and brake (they're the one control) and that my reaction time to brake would be quicker because I didn't need to transfer my foot from accelerator to brake. I showed him my driving licence and reminded him that I had passed the same test using hand controls as I had done without hand controls and that the State regarded me as equally safe as a driver. He had run out of suggestions at this stage so I asked to see his manager. He said he would go and consult him and "could he show him my driving licence, please?" I said "of course", and offering it I said: "And would you like to show him my helicopter pilot's licence as well?" He came back 10 minutes later to say that they were dropping my loading and refunding the previous year's loading.

Their "disabled drivers" loading disappeared entirely after that and I guess they're happy they got away with it for so long. Not long afterwards, an American insurance company entered the market offering a 20 per cent discount to all disabled drivers.

Another funny story was told to me by the late Jack Gilroy. Jack was a legend in Dublin, having won All-Ireland winners medals with the Dublin football team. I did a lot of work for Independent Newspapers over the years buying and selling buildings and I became pally with Jack. He had started out as an apprentice printer and rose through the ranks to become production director for the group and was also appointed to the board. Our last achievement together was when we worked on developing the dramatic glass-fronted building housing the printing presses on the Naas Road. Sadly in the last few years of his career Jack lost both of his legs below the knee due to circulatory problems. We really were kindred spirits and I was able to offer advice and help. One day over lunch through fits of laughing Jack told me the story of how he had been back in his wheelchair due to problems with his stumps but had continued working. He was determined to attend an important AGM of Independent Newspapers which was being held in the Gresham Hotel. He put on his very best suit and tie and his wife Pat dropped him at the hotel and arranged to collect him later. After the meeting Jack rang Pat to say he was ready and to make things easier he wheeled himself out onto O'Connell Street and waited outside the hotel. He had been sitting there for just minutes when a man walking by shoved a five euro note into Jack's top pocket. This was an extremely successful businessman on the board of one of Ireland's most successful companies in his best suit. Just because he was in a wheelchair a man assumed he was begging. Isn't it amazing.

Long before I needed a wheelchair I used to admire a young man in south Dublin whom I regularly used to see whizzing around, on and off paths and on and off buses and trains as he went about his business. I never saw anyone as agile and mobile in a wheelchair. He tells the story of an evening he went into town to go to the cinema. He got the train to Tara Street, bought a can of Coca-Cola and wheeled up to O'Connell Bridge taking the odd sip of Coke. He was on the traffic island on O'Connell Bridge waiting for the pedestrian lights when a passerby stopped and put a coin into his can of Coke.

Years ago I also began to notice that every now and then when I was reversing into a disabled driver's parking space a passing motorist would start blaring their horn, gesticulating and shaking their fist at me. After a while I realised what was happening. Because I was driving an upmarket, newish car, they assumed that I couldn't be a "disabled driver" entitled to use the space. In their minds a disabled driver should be driving a Robin Reliant or some very small, old car. Interesting, isn't it?

Overall, I think the "does he take sugar" phenomenon is fading slowly but there is still a lot of prejudice and ignorance at large. I would love it if this book helped in any way.

// CHAPTER 22 //
ESPECIALLY FOR YOUNGER PEOPLE

For many years I have enjoyed speaking at a number of schools and offering some advice and experience to those nearing the end of their school years. I developed a fondness for Ballinteer Community School in Dublin where the principal at the time, Sister Loreto Ryan, invited me to speak after she saw me on 'The Late Late Show'. The school always went out of its way to cater for students with disabilities and has a higher proportion of pupils with disabilities than most, so I was particularly glad to help over the years. I have spoken at many schools including expensive private ones but I was always particularly touched by the bundles of "thank you" letters which the Ballinteer students sent.

Every single word of advice in this book applies to you as a younger person whether still in school or if you have recently started a job or college. You are at such an important stage of your life and remember that enthusiasm for life and a can-do positive attitude are your most valuable assets. Never let anyone tell you that you cannot succeed because you can achieve anything you want. If you want it badly enough and you are prepared to put in the work, then everything is possible. If you are facing exams then a plan, a timetable for your study, will be your greatest asset. Break down all those daunting subjects into small bites and work your way through them one at a time.

When I was 16 and in Leaving Cert year I was not working well at all. I was too interested in football and socialising. With just a few months to go, the teachers were complaining of my lack of effort and immaturity. Fortunately my father Jim, himself a teacher, sat me down with a large sheet of cardboard. Written in block capitals across the top was "Operation Success". The sheet was a timetable onto which we broke down each subject into study periods. It wasn't anything over-demanding but once the subjects were broken down into parts it didn't look so daunting. One copy of the sheet was stuck on my bedroom wall and another in the kitchen. I stuck to the plan and began to get a bit of a kick out of crossing off parts of the syllabus after I had covered them. The result was that I got a far better Leaving Certificate than anyone (or I) expected. "Operation Success" had lived up to its name in just three months. (You can see where I get some of my ideas.)

For those looking to get a job in a particular company or a particular college course which involves an interview I encourage you to start laying the foundations for that while still in school. Transition Year is an ideal time. Remember that you are trying to make it easy for your interviewer to pick you, you can help him by standing out. I have sat through many hours of interviewing student job applicants and after five or six in a row, it becomes difficult to remember who was who – so differentiate yourself. If you are interested in a particular company then start to show that now. For example let's say that company has a number of shops or offices. Then visit a few branches, have a look around and write down any thoughts. Are they all equally well laid out? Is there a seat or two for customers to rest? Do you know of a town where this company has no outlet at the moment? Compose your thoughts carefully.

Do some googling and find out who does what at the company. Then write a very polite hardcopy letter to that person, perhaps it's the managing director. Always compliment them on their business, tell them who you are and that you have a great interest in their company. You might start by asking if you would be permitted to look around the company headquarters or warehouse. You might politely say that you believe that a particular outlet would benefit from a seat or two for customers. You might suggest that they consider locating in a particular area as you believe there is a good demand there for their goods/services. You might ask if you could briefly meet someone in the company who would tell you more about their staff training. The possibilities are endless.

The likelihood is that you will receive a letter back from the company thanking you for your interest and suggestions and probably agreeing to help you further. If you don't get a response try another individual there. You might do a small project on how the company markets itself in your area. Are they on Facebook? Linked-In? Maybe suggest to them that they create a page or engage in some online marketing to stimulate more "likes" and followers. Always be polite, respectful and enthusiastic.

Over the next year or so keep a little contact going with the company and you'll soon have a few letters from them and you'll know some people there. Now imagine the job interview when it arises; dozens of applicants and all with similar qualifications and abilities. When you are asked at the interview what you know about the company you produce a file of letters and can say that you have been in correspondence with Mr. Bloggs over the last couple of years on their locations, service or marketing and have inspected premises and met several staff etc, etc. Now, you are differentiating yourself and all other things being equal you will get that job. Never forget the power of a polite and well-written, hardcopy letter. Most senior business people like responding to and helping young people.

POSITIVE STROKES

You must appreciate, respect and thank your parents and teachers for their efforts. They deserve your appreciation but they probably don't expect it because we all fall into the habit of taking things for granted. A positive stroke is when you show that appreciation. Your parents are working hard to keep your family going in tough economic circumstances. They are under pressure, tired and stressed. Imagine the impact on your mother if she comes in from work one evening exhausted but instead of her usual evenings toil, you greet her with a big hug and a smile.

"Hi, Mum, how are you? Go in and sit by the fire. I've already lit it and I'll bring you in a cuppa." And as you steer her in, you add: "And Mum, I just want you to know that I love you and we all appreciate how much work you do for us. And I've done the hoovering too."

The surge of joy and warmth your mother will experience will be tremendous. She will be re-energised and delighted to see your new found maturity and responsibility. It's the right thing to do and your new level of maturity will stand to you the next time there's a debate about a particular party or a coming home time. So keep stringing these little moments of thanks and appreciation together and everyone's life will be better.

Similarly, imagine you genuinely thanked your teacher after a class that you found particularly interesting. They'll be amazed. They'll feel great and they'll put even more effort into the next class. It's a win-win situation and everyone's happier. People like to be appreciated and thanked.

STAND OUT

Always have absolute respect for yourself and others. Address your elders as Mister or Missus until they tell you otherwise. Open doors for women and people older than you. Give up your seat on a bus or train. Be five minutes early for your appointments and you will stand out.

Most people over 40 have some difficulty understanding the very fast slurred speech of today's younger generation. Older people, who may have hearing difficulties, have huge problems understanding younger people. Slow down your speech and speak clearly especially in an interview and when you are dealing with people in a work setting.

ALCOHOL

You are at a one in 10 risk of wrecking your life because you drink alcohol. Now I know that such a risk factor has no effect on younger people who believe they are invincible. But just like other illnesses such as cancers, heart disease or allergies there is a very strong genetic link in addiction to alcohol. If there is alcoholism in your family you have a one in three chance of becoming an alcoholic. Those are lousy odds against messing up your life.

Have you found that you are losing touch with one or two of your old friends? They seem to have become a bit boring spending a lot of their time on work or study? You've settled in with some new sets of friends who are much more fun, lots of partying and hanging out. Has someone in your family or perhaps someone you thought was a good friend started to annoy you because they think you're drinking too much? Yes? You're probably already an alcoholic. Your addiction to alcohol is deadly dangerous as you will be the very last person to realise it. That will be long after you have wreaked havoc on everyone and everything that you thought was most important to you. Never excuse how much you drink by telling yourself that you're just the same as your friends because you're friends are probably alcoholics too. Heavy drinkers associate with heavy drinkers. That's one of the tricks that alcohol will play on you.

Another trick alcohol will play on you is to tell you that you deserve a few drinks to relax because of all the hard work and stress in your life or the grief you're getting from your boyfriend/girlfriend or family. In fact, almost certainly, the big problems in your life are caused by your drinking in the first place. See how cunning alcohol is? It turns everything upside down, it depresses you and it chemically changes the way you think. You can't see the wood for the trees. Stop drinking for six months and see if your problems sort themselves out. They probably will. If you couldn't be bothered stopping for six months then you have just proved the point.

In the business world alcohol is widely used in entertaining but you must be careful to keep your wits about you. I have seen a few instances in my time of younger people drinking too much and behaving inappropriately, getting sick or doing or saying something stupid that they would never do when sober. Your younger pals will think you're great fun but your bosses and clients will be embarrassed. While some might give you a chance you may fatally damage your career and reputation with others. Over time you'll realise that it's usually the same people making these mistakes and they are already alcoholics. There's a "self-destruct" part to alcoholism and another trick it plays is to compel its victim to produce their worst behaviour at the very worst imaginable time, i.e. when it will do most damage.

You will also come across people who – only when drinking – will criticise other firms or colleagues. Another character is the one who talks too much when drinking and can't stop himself giving away all sorts of information. Don't become one of those characters.

Don't underestimate or make assumptions about someone because of their background or appearance; you will often be wrong. Never run down your competitors in business. In conversation with anyone, your competitors should be described as a very good company. An experienced client will know whether they are or not and on hearing you he will see great maturity in you. Your job is to make sure he realises that you are better.

SMOKING

Just don't. If you smoke, you have a 50 per cent chance of dying an early, slow and painful death. If you smoke you smell awful. If you smoke you taste awful. If you smoke you are wasting money. If you smoke you don't look cool – you look stupid.

OTHER DRUGS

Don't even try them. Be smart. Be cool.

If you have any worries at all about your drinking or use of drugs, then ask for help and you can get back on the rails. You will be one of the many thousands of people with the exact same problems as you. The sooner you ask for help the better.

You can get help through alcoholicsanonymous.ie or addictionireland.ie or start by having a chat with your doctor. If a friend of yours or someone in your family is drinking too much and you don't know what to do you can get help from Al-Anon or Alateen at al-anon-ireland.org.

To summarise, as regards Drink, Drugs and Smoking – just be very, very careful. You are dicing with death.

A FINAL THOUGHT

In Ireland and the UK, we see young western Europeans as the epitome of style. They are very interested in their appearance, their clothes, their music, their fashion, their image. They hang about cafes, clubs and wine bars with their trendy scooters parked outside and we see them as "cool". Yet they have no great interest in alcohol and they see someone drunk as someone to be scorned and pitied – especially if it's a girl. Being drunk is the most uncool thing you can do. Only in Ireland and the UK is binge-drinking and getting drunk seen as some type of achievement. We call this a cultural drink problem.

// CHAPTER 23 //
TAKING STOCK

I can remember those months in the Burns Unit as if they were yesterday yet so much has happened since then. Thirty years have passed, and I turned 50 this May. Each of those years has brought its own mixture of successes, happiness, mistakes and sadness. I learned to walk again and fought my way back in the world of business. I married and I have three fantastic children, who are happy and healthy. Last year my beautiful mother, Pauline, died in my arms. I have seen friends and neighbours die young through illness and accidents. After 25 years of hard work I became comfortably off. After the sale of the company which I had helped to build I became wealthy by most standards. I have experienced the breakdown of my marriage and entirely fairly, I am no longer so wealthy. From 2006 or so, I experienced continuous breakdowns of the grafted skin on my left stump, with subsequent infections. Where antibiotics used to do the trick in a week, the advent of MRSA had changed all that and caused me terrible trouble. I had four more operations to repair grafts.

A consultant at the National Rehabilitation Hospital called me in and read me the riot act. I could not keep going at the pace I was, continually breaking down grafts which had not been given enough time to heal and repeatedly turning up with MRSA infections expecting the hospital to keep curing them. I had already experienced septicaemia where the infection gets into your bloodstream. She warned me that the next major infection could see me lose my remaining knee which would have a drastic effect on my mobility. In fact, another septicaemia could be fatal. After some deliberation, another breakdown of the graft made my mind up for me and I retired from the property business and changed course. Stopping full-time work allowed my skin to heal properly although it took two more six week periods back in my wheelchair. This time around though I wasn't going to be confined to barracks and I was strong enough to go out socialising and to have my children push me around the supermarket doing the shopping. Needs must. The consultant was right.

Instead of running myself into the ground, now when I saw my skin becoming worn I stopped walking on it for a few days and prevented it breaking down – instead of sticking a plaster on it and hoping for the best as I had done for 25 years. I'm glad to say now that my grafts are in great condition and I haven't had MRSA for over five years.

It's a very good thing that I need to work to pay the bills again. In hindsight, the period after I retired, between my health problems and suddenly being out of the business world, was not a particularly happy one. Like most of us I believe I am happiest when I am working and busy and coming home with a sense of achievement. I think we all need that. I am thoroughly enjoying building up my own little business in advising companies on many of the subjects in this book and as a speaker at conferences and after-dinner events.

And 'being Bono' fills the gaps.

I've reinvented myself as many have had to do because of the recession. I'm still making mistakes and sometimes I have to kick myself into more action but I'm using my plan of 'Small Steps' and making progress on all fronts. The writing and publication of 'Small Steps' sees one of my goals achieved. I became fascinated with the whole area of MRSA and antibiotic resistant bacteria. I researched it heavily and used that knowledge in a thriller I've written called 'The Manhattan Project'. After one near miss with an international publisher and the requisite number of rejections from literary agents that goal is behind schedule. I'm going to have to dig deeper and start afresh. This time I'll make certain it happens.

I am very happy. I have been fortunate and the lucky breaks far outweigh the bad ones. The change of direction in the last few years allowed me the flexibility to maximise my time with my children and my parents. You can't buy that time back and I treasure it. I was blessed to meet a beautiful and talented woman who for some reason is attracted to a legless, separated man with baggage, who pretends he's Bono, and she lifts my heart.

Losing my legs changed my life and it changed me. From a low point of being anointed in the Burns Unit I somehow found the strength to battle my way back. At the heart of that I think was a determination that I was not going to let this disaster get the better of me. I didn't want anyone's pity. I was determined to prove to everyone and myself that I could get back to being "as good" as I was before. I also felt a need to do really well to help my parents who of course were devastated. While there were many setbacks along the way (and will be in the future), I never gave up and I tried even harder.

Gradually over the years I surprised everyone at what I could achieve. I realised the powerful effect of this motivation of working towards a goal and I began to apply it in other areas of my life. It's interesting how aged 20 I was cruising along convinced that I was working extremely hard and that it would be a real challenge to work my way up through the company. And on top of all that, I had the "unfairness" of having to do my Chartered Surveying degree at night by correspondence. Yet, amputate my legs and I was still able to do it. I am convinced that we all have a lot more potential and strengths than we think. Strengths and abilities that we never use because we don't have to use them and as we cruise along we may not discover that they are there. I learned how to make money and I learned how to survive recessions. I learned humility and I have plenty to be humble about. I learned not to be ashamed of being disabled.

Please think about my story of learning to fly. As a perfectly fit 18-year-old I didn't follow my dream to fly because I thought it was beyond me. Twenty years later and now with no legs I set out to become a pilot, *knowing* that I would achieve it even though the task was now surely a 100 times more difficult. Look at the powerful effect my change of mindset had. What changed my mindset was that my legs had been burnt off. That gives you one hell of a new perspective on life. I was now forced into a position where I had to prove to myself and others that I could still do all of the things I had done before when I had legs. One after another I knocked down every obstacle in my way. Some things I had to do a little differently but I could still get the end result. Gradually over the years with a trail of obstacles behind me I realised that I could achieve virtually anything I wanted.

Almost every journalist that interviewed me over those years has asked me one identical question: "Do you think you would have been as successful if you hadn't lost your legs?" I always answered, "Yes". I was happy to simply demonstrate that someone without legs could do a job just as well as someone with legs.

In hindsight I was wrong. I now realise that losing my legs motivated me to prove to myself, and to the people writing me off that I could be just as good as before. In achieving that I learnt the power of motivation, of a positive attitude and of goal-setting. I proved to myself that I could achieve anything I wanted no matter what the obstacles. I have continued to use that power to achieve things that are possibly beyond what I would have achieved had I not discovered that insight and power.

I lost my fear of failure. When your legs have been burnt off there isn't a whole lot more to be afraid of. It gives you a new perspective on life. I "go for" things I might have been afraid to contemplate before. This life is short and we owe it to ourselves to "go for" our dreams.

Sometimes people tell me that the story of how I overcame my disability is "inspirational". If I can help other people in their lives then that is great but I absolutely refuse any credit for that. That is because what I have done has been for myself; for my own benefit. This point struck me forcefully many years ago. I had been asked by a bank to present their annual "Achievement Awards". One by one the recipients were announced and I listened to what they were doing. There was a physiotherapist who had worked for two years in a leper colony, nurses who worked in diabolical conditions in famine regions, a woman who had adopted two severely handicapped children and others. These people were dedicated to helping others and had forgotten about themselves whereas my efforts were all for myself.

I felt like a fraud.

I try to help others and give them the benefit of my experience as much as I can. It's the least I can do. Fairly regularly I am asked by some of the hospitals to visit a young person who has had an amputation or is facing one and I'm glad to do that not least because someone did it for me in Dr. Steevens. I know that this is a help to the patient and their family. One mother wrote to me after I visited her son and told me I was "an angel sent to lift their spirits".

I have found myself in very unusual situations including being in strangers' sitting rooms and taking down my trousers to show how artificial legs work. One Christmas Eve I found myself talking to a young man through his bedroom door. He had had his leg amputated, had been allowed home for Christmas and had locked himself in his room for days. I knew exactly how he felt. One Christmas I was at a party and a man asked if he could speak privately to me. In the hallway he held my hand and with tears in his eyes said he wanted to thank me for saving his life as he had been on the verge of suicide the night he saw me interviewed on 'The Late Late Show' and he had decided to start life afresh. These reactions surprise me and, of course, it is a valuable thing if I can help others by default. But the real thanks must go to those who dedicate themselves to helping others at a great cost to their own lives. I don't do that. Any efforts are for my own benefit and that's very different.

I hope that you have enjoyed reading these stories, experiences and ideas and that they have given you food for thought. I look forward to the next 50 years of opportunities and setbacks with great hope, with positivity and with joy. Everything is possible. Advance with calm.

// ACKNOWLEDGEMENTS //

Not many writers are lucky enough to have an English teacher and academic author as a father, and I am grateful to my dad, Jim, for his advice and support. Many of the more mature readers will remember having Jim McNeive's book "An Economic History of Ireland" in their schoolbag for their Leaving Certificate.

A couple of years ago, I met up for a coffee with an old friend, Donal Egan, who is an expert on customer service and sales. I was telling him about writing my "thriller". He was encouraging, of course, but as only old friends can, Donal said: "Eh Paul, if you don't mind me saying so, the first book you should be writing is about your life and about your ideas on business." He then listed off a number of topics he thought I should cover. The more I thought about it, the more I realised that he was right, and so I embarked on "Small Steps". So, thank you Donal, for your blunt advice.

I want to acknowledge the support, expertise and hard work of my publishers, Ballpoint Press, and it was so encouraging to see their instant enthusiasm for my book. In particular, my editor at Ballpoint, P.J. Cunningham has drastically improved the text and dragged memories and emotions from me which I had never thought of writing about. Also at Ballpoint, my thanks to Rosemary for her rock solid advice on the publishing business and to Clara, for keeping us all on our toes.

For keeping me walking, dancing, singing and working, I pay tribute to everyone at the National Rehabilitation Hospital and in particular, Dr. Frank Keane, Dr. Angela McNamara, Dr. Nicola Ryall, Paddy Brock, the late Jimmy McKenzie, Charles Murray, Ability Matters, and to the physios and nursing staff for their skill and help over the years. Henry Murdoch, Chairman of the Hospital Board and Derek Greene, the Chief Executive of the Hospital have been of great support.

I also owe a debt to the A&E unit at Loughlinstown Hospital and the Burns Unit at the former Dr. Steevens Hospital, who between them saved my life. Kevin Carroll, formerly of the NRH, and now Vice President at Hanger Prosthetics and his colleague Dan Strzempka, have been of enormous help to me. Mr. Denis Lawlor, who did all of my skin grafting in 1982, remains my first port of call for any skin problems.

In the business world, people who have helped me tremendously over the years include Ian French, Larry Brennan, Angus Potterton and Ronan O'Driscoll at Savills and Tom Dunne at DIT, Bolton Street. Michael Cotter of Park Developments and James Carroll were great clients and are still friends.

I am very proud of my beautiful children, Megan, Killian and Michael, a great credit to their Mother and who are such a joy in my life and make everything worthwhile.

Thank you to my many loyal friends, for your help and support over the years, especially when times are tough, and especially Rory Power and his fantastic wife Caroline, who is an inspiration to me.

Lastly to my sisters Sheila and Helen who have always been a great support.

Thank you all.

Paul McNeive
September 2012

// INDEX //

For further information on Paul McNeive's work as a
Business Consultant and Speaker, see PaulMcNeive.com

For information on hiring Hugh Toohy –
The World's Greatest Rockstar, see HughToohy.com